GOD'S NO AND GOD'S YES

The Proper Distinction Between Law and Gospel

GOD'S NO AND GOD'S YES
The Proper Distinction Between Law and Gospel

C. F. W. WALTHER

Condensed by Walter C. Pieper

CPH.
SAINT LOUIS

Concordia Publishing House, St. Louis, Missouri

INTRODUCTION

The Proper Distinction Between Law and Gospel is a student transcript of C. F. W. Walther's Friday evening "Luther Hour" lectures delivered between Sept. 12, 1884, and Nov. 6, 1885. Walther, as professor of theology at Concordia Seminary, St. Louis, felt it his duty not only to make clear to his students the meaning of the doctrines of the Sacred Scriptures, but also "to talk the doctrine into their hearts" so that as pastors they would be able to "come forward as living witnesses with a demonstration of the Spirit and of power."

Walther covered a variety of topics in the Luther Hour lectures. He spoke on the Inspiration of the Scriptures, the Truth of the Christian Religion, Secret Societies, Justification, Predestination and Justification, Luther's "Large Confession on the Blessed Sacrament," and two series on the Proper Distinction Between Law and Gospel. The first series on the Law and the Gospel was presented in 1878 in 13 theses. This series was published in 1893. The second series included 25 theses and was published in 1897. An English translation of this series was made by W. H. T. Dau and was published in 1929. This book is a condensation of Dau's translation.

C. F. W. Walther carefully prepared his material for presentation. However, careful as he was about an oral presentation, he was even more careful about his printed work. In preparation for printing, he reworked his orally presented material so that the reader was given the best possible product. Since *The Proper Distinction Between Law and Gospel* was published posthumously, Walther did not have the opportunity to rework his lectures and prepare them for publication as was his practice. If he had, the style of the work would, without a doubt, have been different. Much of the material within this work was extemporaneous, spoken to people close to him. Dau says in the Preface and Introduction to his translation of the work: "Moreover, a greater freedom, even a certain abandon, is quite acceptable when an old, beloved professor is talking to an audience made up almost entirely of his students." In this way we receive the bonus of becoming acquainted with Walther the pastor of theological students, as well as with his theology.

The importance of the proper distinction between the Law and the Gospel is shown by Walther's two lecture series on the topic, the publication of both series, and the early translation of the second series into English. The effect of *The Proper Distinction Between Law and Gospel* cannot easily be measured; however, all who list the contributions which Walther made to the church include this work. It could be argued that this was his greatest contribution to the church, for within Lutheranism pastoral practice in preaching, counseling, and evaluating the mission of the church have grown out of the understanding of the proper distinction between the Law and the Gospel.

C. F. W. Walther's *The Proper Distinction Between Law and Gospel* is a classic; to condense it is hazardous. We have taken the risk in the hope of introducing this work to a wider audience, for it provides many fresh insights and correctives. The goal of the condensation is to create new interest in the complete work. To this end, we have made Walther speak for himself, eliminating the extensive quotes from the Lutheran Confessions, Martin Luther, and the dogmaticians. Since this work is the product of Luther Hour lectures, most of the non-Biblical quotations are from Luther, many of which are not readily available in English translation. To unify the presentation of the various theses, we have eliminated the original's division by lectures, and have instead dealt with each thesis as a unit. In selecting material to be retained under each of the theses, we have attempted to use that which most directly relates to the particular thesis under discussion.

LAW AND GOSPEL

Thesis I

The doctrinal contents of the entire Holy Scriptures, both of the Old and the New Testament, are made up of two doctrines differing fundamentally from each other, viz., the Law and the Gospel.

Thesis II

Only he is an orthodox teacher who not only presents all the articles of faith in accordance with Scripture, but also rightly distinguishes from each other the Law and the Gospel.

Thesis III

Rightly distinguishing the Law and the Gospel is the most difficult and the highest art of Christians in general and of theologians in particular. It is taught only by the Holy Spirit in the school of experience.

Thesis IV

The true knowledge of the distinction between the Law and the Gospel is not only a glorious light, affording the correct understanding of the entire Holy Scriptures, but without this knowledge Scripture is and remains a sealed book.

Thesis V

The first manner of confounding Law and Gospel is the one most easily recognized—and the grossest. It is adopted, for instance, by Papists, Socinians, and Rationalists and consists in this, that Christ is represented as a new Moses, or Lawgiver, and the Gospel turned into a doctrine of meritorious works, while at the same time those who teach that the Gospel is the message of the free grace of God in Christ are condemned and anathematized, as is done by the papists.

Thesis VI

In the second place, the Word of God is not rightly divided when the Law is not preached in its full sternness and the Gospel not in its full sweetness, when, on the contrary, Gospel elements are mingled with the Law and Law elements with the Gospel.

Thesis VII

In the third place, the Word of God is not rightly divided when the Gospel is preached first and then the Law; sanctification first and then justification; faith first and then repentance; good works first and then grace.

Thesis VIII

In the fourth place, the Word of God is not rightly divided when the Law is preached to those who are already in terror on account of their sins, or the Gospel to those who live securely in their sins.

Thesis IX

In the fifth place, the Word of God is not rightly divided when sinners who have been struck down and terrified by the Law are directed, not to the Word and the Sacraments, but to their own prayers and wrestlings with God in order that they may win their way into a state of grace; in other words, when they are told to keep on praying and struggling until they feel that God has received them into grace.

Thesis X

In the sixth place, the Word of God is not rightly divided when the preacher describes faith in a manner as if the mere inert acceptance of truths, even while a person is living in mortal sins, renders that person righteous in the sight of God and saves him; or as if faith makes a person righteous and saves him for the reason that it produces in him love and reformation of his mode of living.

Thesis XI

In the seventh place, the Word of God is not rightly divided when there is a disposition to offer the comfort of the Gospel only to those who have been made contrite by the Law, not from fear of the wrath and punishment of God, but from love of God.

Thesis XII

In the eighth place, the Word of God is not rightly divided when the preacher represents contrition alongside of faith as a cause of the forgiveness of sin.

Thesis XIII

In the ninth place, the Word of God is not rightly divided when one makes an appeal to believe in a manner as if a person could make himself believe or at least help towards that end, instead of preaching faith into a person's heart by laying the Gospel promises before him.

Thesis XIV

In the tenth place, the Word of God is not rightly divided when faith is required as a condition of justification and salvation, as if a person were righteous in the sight of God and saved, not only by faith, but also on account of his faith, for the sake of his faith, and in view of his faith.

Thesis XV

In the eleventh place, the Word of God is not rightly divided when the Gospel is turned into a preaching of repentance.

Thesis XVI

In the twelfth place, the Word of God is not rightly divided when the preacher tries to make people believe that they are truly converted as soon as they have become rid of certain vices and engage in certain works of piety and virtuous practises.

Thesis XVII

In the thirteenth place, the Word of God is not rightly divided when a description is given of faith, both as regards its strength and the consciousness and productiveness of it, that does not fit all believers at all times.

Thesis XVIII

In the fourteenth place, the Word of God is not rightly divided when the universal corruption of mankind is described in such a manner as to create the impression that even true believers are still under the spell of ruling sins and are sinning purposely.

Thesis XIX

In the fifteenth place, the Word of God is not rightly divided when the preacher speaks of certain sins as if they were not of a damnable, but of a venial nature.

Thesis XX

In the sixteenth place, the Word of God is not rightly divided when a person's salvation is made to depend on his association with the visible orthodox Church and when salvation is denied to every person who errs in any article of faith.

Thesis XXI

In the seventeenth place, the Word of God is not rightly divided when men are taught that the Sacraments produce salutary effects ex opere operato, *that is, by the mere outward performance of a sacramental act.*

Thesis XXII

In the eighteenth place, the Word of God is not rightly divided when a false distinction is made between a person's being awakened and his being converted; moreover, when a person's inability to believe is mistaken for his not being permitted to believe.

Thesis XXIII

In the nineteenth place, the Word of God is not rightly divided when an attempt is made by means of the demands or the threats or the promises of the Law to induce the unregenerate to put away their sins and engage in good works and thus become godly; on the other hand, when an endeavor is made, by means of the commands of the Law rather than by the admonitions of the Gospel, to urge the regenerate to do good.

Thesis XXIV

In the twentieth place, the Word of God is not rightly divided when the unforgiven sin against the Holy Ghost is described in a manner as if it could not be forgiven because of its magnitude.

Thesis XXV

In the twenty-first place, the Word of God is not rightly divided when the person teaching it does not allow the Gospel to have a general predominance in his teaching.

The Proper Distinction Between Law and Gospel

If you are to become efficient teachers in our churches and schools, it is a matter of indispensable necessity that you have a most minute knowledge of all doctrines of the Christian revelation. However, what is needed over and above your knowledge of the doctrines is that you know how to apply them correctly. You must not only have a clear apperception of the doctrines in your intellect, but all of them must have entered deeply into your heart and there manifested their divine, heavenly power. All these doctrines must have become so precious, so valuable, so dear to you, that you cannot but profess with a glowing heart in the words of Paul: "We believe, and so we speak," and in the words of all the apostles: "We cannot but speak of what we have seen and heard."

Of all doctrines the foremost is the doctrine of justification. However, second in importance is *how Law and Gospel are to be divided.*

Luther says that he is willing to place him who is well versed in the art of dividing the Law from the Gospel at the head of all and call him a doctor of Holy Writ. But I would not have you believe that I intend to place myself ahead of everybody else and be regarded as a doctor of the Sacred Scriptures. For myself I rather wish to remain a humble disciple and sit at the feet of Dr. Luther, to learn this doctrine from him even as he learned it from the apostles and prophets.

Comparing Holy Scripture with other writings, we observe that no book is apparently so full of contradictions as the Bible, and that, not only in minor points, but in the principal matter, in the doctrine how we may come to God and be saved. In one place the Bible offers forgiveness to all sinners; in another place forgiveness of sins is withheld from all sinners. In one passage a free offer of life everlasting is made to all men; in another, men are directed to do something themselves towards being saved. This riddle is solved when we reflect that there are in the Scriptures two entirely different doctrines, the doctrine of the Law and the doctrine of the Gospel.

Thesis I

The doctrinal contents of the entire Holy Scriptures, both of the Old and the New Testament, are made up of two doctrines differing fundamentally from each other, viz., the Law and the Gospel.

The point of difference between the Law and the Gospel is not that the Gospel is a divine and the Law a human doctrine. Not at all; whatever of either doctrine is contained in the Scriptures is the Word of the living God Himself.

Nor is this the difference, that only the Gospel is necessary, not the Law, as if the latter were a mere addition that could be dispensed with. Both are equally necessary. Without the Law the Gospel is not understood; without the Gospel the Law benefits us nothing.

Nor can this distinction be admitted, that the Law is the teaching of the Old while the Gospel is the teaching of the New Testament. There are Gospel contents in the Old and Law contents in the New Testament.

Nor do the Law and the Gospel differ as regards their final aim, as though the Gospel aimed at men's salvation, the Law at men's condemnation. Both have for their final aim man's salvation; only the Law, ever since the Fall, cannot lead us to salvation; it can only prepare us for the Gospel. Furthermore, it is through the Gospel that we obtain the ability to fulfil the Law to a certain extent.

Nor can we establish a difference by claiming that the Law and the Gospel contradict each other. There are no contradictions in Scripture. Each is distinct from the other, but both are in the most perfect harmony with one another.

Finally, the difference is not this, that only one of these doctrines is meant for Christians. Even for the Christian the Law still retains its significance. Indeed, when a person ceases to employ either of these two doctrines, he is no longer a true Christian.

The true points of difference between the Law and the Gospel are the following: —

1. These two doctrines differ as regards the *manner of* their *being revealed* to man;

2. As regards their *contents;*

3. As regards the *promises* held out by either doctrine;

4. As regards their *threatenings;*

5. As regards the *function* and the *effect* of either doctrine;

6. As regards the *persons* to whom either the one or the other doctrine must be preached.

In the first place, Law and Gospel differ as regards *the manner of their being revealed to man.* Man was created with the Law written in his heart. In consequence of the Fall this script in the heart has become quite dulled, but it has not been utterly wiped out. The Law may be preached to the most ungodly person, and his conscience will tell him, That is true. But when the Gospel is preached to him, his conscience does not tell him the same. The preaching of the Gospel rather makes him angry. The worst slave of vice admits that he ought to do what is written in the Law. Why is this? Because the Law is written in his heart. The situation is different when the Gospel is preached. The Gospel reveals and proclaims free acts of divine grace; and these are not self-evident. What God has done according to the Gospel He was not obliged to do.

The second point of difference between the Law and the Gospel is shown by the *contents* of either. The Law tells us what we are to do. The Gospel reveals to us only what God is doing. The Law speaks concerning our works; the Gospel, concerning the great works of God. In the Law we hear the tenfold summons, "Thou shalt." The Gospel, on the other hand, makes no demands whatever. The Law has nothing to say about forgiveness, about grace. It issues only commands and demands. The Gospel, on the other hand, only makes offers. It contains nothing but grace and truth!

Law and Gospel differ, in the third place, by reason of their *promises.* What the Law promises is just as great as what the Gospel promises, namely, everlasting life and salvation. But at this point we are confronted with a mighty difference: All promises of the Law are made on the condition that we fulfill the Law perfectly. Accordingly, the promises of the Law are the more disheartening, the greater they are. The Law offers us food, but does not hand it down to us where we can reach it. It says to us indeed: "I will quench the thirst of your soul and appease your hunger." But it is not able to accomplish this because it always adds: "All this you shall have if you do what I command."

Over and against this note the language of the Gospel. It promises us the grace of God and salvation without any condition whatsoever. It is a promise of free grace. It asks nothing of us but this, "Take what

16

I give, and you have it." That is not a condition, but a kind invitation.

The fourth difference between the Law and the Gospel relates to *threats*. The Gospel contains no threats at all, but only words of consolation. Wherever in Scripture you come across a threat, you may be assured that that passage belongs in the Law, for the Law is nothing but threats.

The fifth point of difference between the Law and the Gospel concerns the *effects* of these two doctrines. The effect of the preaching of the Law is threefold. In the first place, the Law tells us what to do, but does not enable us to comply with its commands; it rather causes us to become more unwilling to keep the Law.

In the second place, the Law uncovers to man his sins, but offers him no help to get out of them and thus hurls man into despair.

In the third place, the Law produces contrition. It conjures up the terrors of hell, of death, of the wrath of God. But is has not a drop of comfort to offer the sinner.

The effects of the Gospel are of an entirely different nature. They consist in this, that, in the first place, the Gospel, when demanding faith, offers and gives us faith in that very demand. When we preach to people: Believe in the Lord Jesus Christ, God gives them faith through our preaching. We preach faith, and any person not willfully resisting obtains faith.

The second effect of the Gospel is that it does not at all reprove the sinner, but takes all terror, all fear, all anguish, from him and fills him with peace and joy in the Holy Ghost.

In the third place, the Gospel does not require anything good that man must furnish: not a good heart, not a good disposition, no improvement of his condition, no godliness, no love either of God or men. It issues no orders, but it changes man. It plants love into his heart and makes him capable of all good works. It demands nothing, but it gives all.

Finally, the sixth point of difference between the Law and the Gospel relates to the *persons* to whom either doctrine is to be preached. The persons on whom either doctrine is to operate, and the end for which it is to operate, are utterly different. The Law is to be preached to secure sinners and the Gospel to alarmed sinners. In other respects both doctrines must indeed be preached, but at this point the question is: Which are the persons to whom the Law must be preached rather than the Gospel? and vice versa.

1 Tim. 1:8-10: As long as a person is at ease in his sins, as long as he is unwilling to quit some particular sin, so long only the Law, which

curses and condemns him, is to be preached to him. However, the moment he becomes frightened at his condition, the Gospel is to be promptly administered to him; for from that moment on he no longer can be classified with secure sinners. Accordingly, while the devil holds you in a *single* sin, you are not yet a proper subject for the Gospel to operate upon; only the Law must be preached to you.

To poor, sad-hearted sinners — I repeat it — not a word of the Law must be preached. Woe to the preacher who would continue to preach the Law to a famished sinner! On the contrary, to such a person the preacher must say: "Do but come! There is still room! No matter how great a sinner you are, there is still room for you. Even if you were a Judas or a Cain, there is still room. Oh, do, do come to Jesus!" Persons of this kind are proper subjects on whom the Gospel is to operate.

Thesis II

Only he is an orthodox teacher who not only presents all the articles of faith in accordance with Scripture, but also rightly distinguishes from each other the Law and the Gospel.

This thesis divides into two parts. The first part states a requisite of an orthodox teacher, *viz.,* that he must present all the articles of faith in accordance with Scripture.

Scripture requires that we have the Word of God absolutely pure and unadulterated and that we be able to say when coming down from the pulpit: "I could take an oath upon it that I have rightly preached the Word of God. Even to an angel coming down from heaven I could say: My preaching has been correct." That explains the paradox remark of Luther that a preacher must not pray the Lord's Prayer when coming down from the pulpit, but that he should do so before the sermon. For an orthodox preacher need not pray after delivering his sermon: "Forgive me my trespasses," since he can say: "I have proclaimed the pure truth."

Suppose someone could truthfully say, "There was no false teaching in my sermon," still his entire sermon may have been wrong. The second part of our thesis says so. Only he is an orthodox teacher who, in addition to other requirements, rightly distinguishes Law and Gospel from each other. That is the final test of a proper sermon. The value of a sermon depends not only on this, that every statement in it be taken from the Word of God and be in agreement with the same, but also on this, whether Law and Gospel have been rightly divided.

It is a wrong application of the Gospel to preach it to such as are not afraid of sinning. On the other hand, an even more horrible situation is created if the pastor is a legalistic teacher, who refuses to preach the Gospel to his congregation because he says: "These people will misuse it anyway." Are poor sinners on that account to be deprived of the Gospel? Let the wicked perish; nevertheless the children of God shall know how near at hand their help is and how easily it is obtained. Anyone withholding the Gospel from such as are in need of consolation fails to divide Law and Gospel.

Thesis III

Rightly distinguishing the Law and the Gospel is the most difficult and the highest art of Christians in general and of theologians in particular. It is taught only by the Holy Spirit in the school of experience.

This thesis does not mean that the doctrine of the Law and the Gospel is so difficult that it cannot be learned without the aid of the Holy Ghost. It is easy — easy enough for children to learn. But at the present time we are studying the *application* and the *use* of this doctrine. The practical application of this doctrine presents difficulties which no man can surmount by reasonable reflections. The Holy Spirit must teach men this in the school of experience. The difficulties of mastering this art confront the minister, in the first place, in so far as he is a Christian; in the second place, in so far as he is a minister.

In the first place, then, the proper distinction between the Law and the Gospel is a difficult and high art to the minister in so far as he is a Christian. Indeed, the proper distinction between the Law and the Gospel is the highest art which a person can learn.

Ps. 51:10-11: David prays God for a right spirit. After his horrible fall, the shedding of innocent blood and the sin of adultery, David had lost assurance of divine grace. Absolution was, indeed, pronounced to him when he had come to a penitent knowledge of his sin, but we do not hear that he forthwith became cheerful. On the contrary, many of his psalms plainly show that he was in very great misery and affliction. When the messenger of God approached him with the declaration: "The Lord also has put away your sin," his heart sighed, "Ah, no! That is not possible." This exalted royal prophet knew the doctrine of the Law and Gospel full well. All his psalms are full of references to the distinction between the two. But when he fell into sin himself, he lacked the practical ability of applying his knowledge. He cried: "Put a new and right spirit within me."

In Luke 5:8 the Lord comes to the disciple whom He had named Petros, a rockman, and bids him and his fellow-fishermen, after an unsuccessful night on the lake, to drop their nets in deep water. Peter complied, most likely expecting, however, that he would catch nothing. But, lo! they caught such a multitude of fishes that their nets broke. Now Peter is seized with fear. He reflects: "That must be the almighty God Himself who has spoken to me. That must be my Maker. He will one day be my Judge!" He falls down at Jesus' knees and says: "Depart from me, for I am a sinful man, O Lord." He expects the Lord to say to him: "Look at the multitude of sins you have committed. You are worthy of everlasting death and damnation." Where, then, did Peter's fright come from? Why did he not thank Jesus when he fell down at His knees? Because his many sins passed before his mind's eye, and in that condition it was impossible for him to express cheerful gratitude, but he had to drop trembling to his knees and cry to his Lord and Savior those awful words: "Depart from me, O Lord." The devil had robbed him of all comfort and whispered to him that he must speak thus to Jesus. He expected nothing else than to be slain by the Lord. He was incapable of distinguishing Law and Gospel. If he had been able to do this, he could have approached Jesus cheerfully, remembering that He had forgiven all his sins.

1 John 3:19-20: When our heart does not condemn us, it is easy to distinguish Law and Gospel. That is the state of a Christian. But he may get into a condition where his heart condemns him. Do what he will, he cannot silence the accusing voice within. Now, if in that moment a person can rightly divide Law and Gospel, he will fall at Jesus' feet and take comfort in Jesus' merit. That, however, is not easy.

After Christians have learned to make the proper practical use of the distinction between the Law and the Gospel, they join St. John in saying: "God is greater than my heart; He has rendered a different verdict on men's sinning, and that applies also to me." Blessed are you if you have learned this difficult art. If you have learned it, do not imagine yourselves perfect. You will always be no more than beginners in this art. Remember this: When the Law condemns you, then immediately lay hold upon the Gospel.

Like two hostile forces, Law and Gospel sometimes clash with each other in a person's conscience. The Gospel says to him: "You have been received into God's grace." The Law says to him: "Do not believe it; for look at your past life. How many and grievous are your sins! Examine the thoughts and desires that you have harbored in your mind." On an occasion like this it is difficult to divide Law and Gospel. When this happens to a person, he must say to the Law: "Away with you! Your demands have all been fully met, and you have nothing to demand of me. There is One who has paid my debt." This difficulty does not occur to a person dead in his trespasses and sins; he is soon through with the Law. But the difficulty is quite real to a person who has been converted.

We now consider that also for *theologians as such* the proper distinction between Law and Gospel is the highest and most difficult art and that everything else that a theologian must know is of less value than this art.

2 Tim. 2:15: The apostle's admonition to Timothy to *do his best* indicates that dividing Law and Gospel properly is a great, difficult art.

Luke 12:42-44: What the Lord terms a great achievement is not the mere recital of the Word of God, or, to stick to the simile, the apportioning of some food to every member of the household, but this, that every one is given his due portion at the proper time, that each one is treated as his spiritual condition requires. This must be done at the proper time. It is a poor steward that gives the servants something now and then allows a long time to pass before he gives them something again and is unconcerned about the quantity of food that he must provide and about the proper time to serve it. The lesson conveyed by this simile is this: A preacher must be well versed in the art of ministering to each in season exactly what he needs, either the Law or the Gospel.

2 Cor. 2:16; 3:4-6: From God alone the apostle expects his qualification for this high and difficult art.

Preach so that every hearer feels: "He means me. He has painted the hypocrite exactly as I am." Again, the pastor may have described a person afflicted with temptation so plainly that the actual victim of a temptation has to admit: "That is my condition." The penitent person must soon feel while listening to the pastor: "That comfort is meant for me; I am to appropriate it." The alarmed soul must be led to think: "Oh, that is a sweet message; that is for me!" Yea, the impenitent, too, must be made to acknowledge: "The preacher has painted my exact portrait."

Accordingly, the preacher must understand how to depict accurately the inward condition of every one of his hearers. A mere objective presentation of the various doctrines is not sufficient to this end. A person may be orthodox, may have perceived the pure doctrine, but he is not in personal communion with God, has not yet settled his account with God, has not yet attained to the assurance that his debt of sins has been remitted.

The difficulty of properly dividing Law and Gospel is still greater in the pastor's private ministrations to individuals. In the pulpit he may say various things, hoping they will strike home. But when people seek his pastoral counsel, he is confronted with a far greater difficulty. He will soon observe which of his callers is a Christian, which not. This is not saying that the pastor may not be deceived by the pious mien and manners of a hypocrite. However, if he can rightly divide Law and Gospel, his callers may have deceived him, but it is their own fault if they applied the wrong teaching to themselves. A fearful responsibility is assumed by the pastor only in case he himself is to blame if his people misunderstand him. If people act like Christians only to deceive me, they deceive themselves rather than me. A pastor must treat any person as a Christian when he appears to be one, and *vice versa*.

However, not all unchristians are alike. One is a crass and scurrilous irreligionist and a scorner of the Bible; another is orthodox and possesses the dead faith of the intellect only. The minister — unless he is himself a slave of sin and incapable of forming a judgment of the person before him — recognizes in the latter a person spiritually blind and still in the bonds of spiritual death. Now, if an unchristian has become truly alarmed and filled with an unnamed dread, though he is still unbroken, the pastor must say to himself: "This person must first be crushed." Some are addicted to a vice, others are self-righteous. To discover to which class these various unconverted persons belong and to apply the proper medicine to them, that is the very difficulty of which I am speaking. My object is to convince you that a preacher can be truly fitted out for his calling only by the Holy Spirit.

Finally, the greatest difficulty is encountered in dealing with true Christians according to their particular spiritual condition. One has a weak, another a strong faith; one is cheerful, another sorrowful; one is sluggish, another burning with zeal; one has only little spiritual knowledge, another is deeply grounded in the truth.

Thesis IV

The true knowledge of the distinction between the Law and the Gospel is not only a glorious light, affording the correct understanding of the entire Holy Scriptures, but without this knowledge Scripture is and remains a sealed book.

While still ignorant of the distinction between the Law and the Gospel, a person receives the impression that a great number of contradictions are contained in the Scriptures; in fact, the entire Scriptures seem to be made up of contradictions. Now the Scriptures pronounce one blessed, now they condemn him. When the rich youth asked the Lord: "What good thing shall I do that I may have eternal life?" the Lord replied: "If you would enter life, keep the commandments." When the jailer at Philippi addressed the identical question to Paul and Silas, he received this answer: "Believe in the Lord Jesus, and you will be saved, you and your household." On the one hand, we read in Hab. 2:4: "The righteous shall live by his faith"; on the other hand, we note that John in his First Epistle (3:7) says: "He who does right is righteous." Over and against this the apostle Paul declares: "Since all have sinned and fall short of the glory of God, they are justified by His grace as a gift, through the redemption which is in Christ Jesus." On the one hand, we note that the Scripture declares God has no pleasure in sinners; on the other hand, we find that it states: "Whoever calls on the name of the Lord shall be saved." In one place Paul cries: "The wrath of God is revealed from heaven against all ungodliness and wickedness of men," and Ps. 5:4 we read: "Thou art not a God who delights in wickedness; evil may not sojourn with Thee"; in another place we hear Peter saying: "Set your hope fully upon the grace that is coming to you." On the one hand, we are told that all the world is under the wrath of God; on the other hand, we read: "God so loved the world that He gave His only Son, that whoever believes in Him should not perish but have eternal life." Another remarkable passage is 1 Cor. 6:9-11, where the apostle first makes this statement: "Neither the immoral, nor idolaters, nor adulterers, nor homosexuals, nor thieves, nor the greedy, nor drunkards, nor revilers, nor robbers will inherit the kingdom of God," and then adds: "And such were some of you. But you were washed, you were sanctified, you were justified in the name of the Lord Jesus Christ and in the Spirit of our God." Must not a person who knows nothing of the distinction between the Law and the Gospel be swallowed up in utter darkness when reading all this? Must he not indignantly cry out: "What? That is to be God's Word? A book full of such contradictions?"

For the situation is not that the Old Testament reveals a wrathful, the New Testament a gracious God, or that the Old Testament teaches salvation by a person's own works, the New Testament, by faith. No; we find both teachings in the Old as well as in the New Testament. But the moment we learn to know the distinction between the Law and the Gospel, it is as if the sun were rising upon the Scriptures, and we behold all the contents of the Scriptures in the most beautiful harmony. We see that the Law was not revealed to us to put the notion into our heads that we can become righteous by it, but to teach us that we are utterly unable to fulfill the Law. When we have learned this, we shall know what a sweet message, what a glorious doctrine, the Gospel is and shall receive it with exuberant joy.

However, the preacher must also be careful not to say that the Law has been abolished; for that is not true. The Law remains in force; it is not abrogated. But we have another message besides that of the Law. God does not say: "Through the Law comes righteousness," but: "Through the Law comes knowledge of sin." Romans says: "To one who . . . trusts Him who justifies *the ungodly*, his faith is reckoned as righteousness." Hence we are on the right way to salvation the moment we are convinced that we are ungodly.

Rom. 10:2-4: The ignorance of the Jews is that "They do not recognize the righteousness that is valid in the sight of God." That is their lack of understanding. They imagined they must be zealots in behalf of the Law; for as it was most assuredly God's law, how might anyone dare depart from it? If they had paid attention to Paul's preaching, they would soon have observed that Paul allowed the Law to remain in force. Seeing that, they would not have become enemies of the Gospel, and the dreadful darkness which settled upon them like the pall of night would have been dispelled.

Thesis V

The first manner of confounding Law and Gospel is the one most easily recognized—and the grossest. It is adopted, for instance, by papists, Socinians, and rationalists and consists in this, that Christ is represented as a new Moses, or lawgiver, and the Gospel turned into a doctrine of meritorious works, while at the same time those who teach that the Gospel is the message of the free grace of God in Christ are condemned and anathematized, as is done by the papists.

The decrees of the Council of Trent speak of the Gospel as containing the doctrines of salvation. However, they add immediately that the Gospel also prescribes morals. That is the interpretation they put on the intention of Christ when He said: "Go ye into all the world and preach the Gospel to every creature" (Mark 16:15). They evidently do not intend to accept the Gospel in the true sense of the word. In the meaning in which they understand it, it is, at best, a law such as Moses proclaimed.

If Christ came into the world to publish new laws to us, He might as well have stayed in heaven. Moses had already given us so perfect a law that we could not fulfill it. Now if Christ had given us additional laws, that would have had to drive us to despair.

The very term *Gospel* contradicts this view. We know that Christ Himself has called His Word *Gospel;* for He says in Mark 16:15: "Go into all the world and preach the *Gospel* to the whole creation." In order that the meaning which He connected with the word *Gospel* might be understood, He states the contents of the Gospel in these concrete terms: "He who believes and is baptized," etc. If the teaching of Christ were a law, it would not be a glad tiding but a sad tiding.

Turning to the Old Testament, we see even there what the character of the teaching of Christ is. We read in Gen. 3:15: "He [the Woman's Seed] shall bruise your head." The Messiah, the Redeemer, the Savior is not to come for the purpose of telling us what we are to do, what works we are to perform in order to escape from the terrible dominion of darkness, sin, and death. These feats the Messiah is not going to leave for us to accomplish, but He will do all that Himself. *"He shall bruise the serpent's head"* means that He shall destroy the kingdom of the devil. All that man has to do is to know that he has been redeemed, that he has been set free from his prison, that he has no more to do than to believe and accept this message and rejoice over it with all his heart. If the text were to read: "He shall save you," that would not be so comforting; or if it read: "You must believe in Him," we should be at a loss to know what is meant by this faith. This First Gospel was the fountain from which the believers in the Old Testament drew their comfort. It was important for them to know: "There is One coming who will not only tell us what we must do to get to heaven. No, the Messiah will do all Himself to bring us there." Now that the rule of the devil has been destroyed, anything that I must do cannot come into consideration. If the devil's dominion is demolished, I am free. There is nothing for me to do but to *appropriate* this to myself. That is what Scripture means when it says, "Believe." That means, Claim as your own what Christ has acquired.

Jer. 31:31-34 God is going to make a *new* covenant. This covenant is not to be a legal covenant like the one which He established with Israel on Mount Sinai. The Messiah will not say: "You must be people of such and such character; your manner of living must be after this or that fashion; you must do such and such works." No such doctrine will be introduced by the Messiah. He writes His Law directly into the heart, so that a person living under Him is a law unto himself. He is not coerced by a force from without, but is urged from within. "For I will forgive their iniquity, and I will remember their sin no more" — these words state the reason for the preceding statement. They are a summary of the Gospel of Christ: forgiveness of sin by the free grace of God, for the sake of Jesus Christ. Any one, therefore, imagining that Christ is a new lawgiver and has brought us new laws cancels the entire Christian religion.

The Christian religion says: "You are a lost and condemned sinner; you cannot be your own Savior. But do not despair on that account. There is One who has acquired salvation for you. Christ has opened the portals of heaven to you and says to you: Come, for all things are ready. Come to the marriage of the Lamb." That is the reason, too, why Christ says: "I heal the sick, not those who are well. I came to seek and to save the lost. I have not come to call the righteous, but sinners to repentance."

Everywhere we see the Lord Jesus surrounded by sinners, and behind Him stand lurking the Pharisees. Sinners, hungering and thirsting, stand round about Him. Though the divine majesty shines forth from Him, they are not afraid to approach Him; they have confidence in Him. The Pharisees utter the bitter reproach: "This man receives sinners and eats with them." The Lord hears the remark. He confirms the truth of their statement, which by them was meant as a reproach, by continuing the censured action, as if He wished to say: "Yes, I want sinners about Me," and then proceeds to prove this by telling the parable of the Lost Sheep. The shepherd picks up the lost sheep, no matter how torn and bruised it is. He places it on his shoulder and, rejoicing, carries it to the sheepfold. The Lord explains His conduct also by the parable of the Lost Piece of Silver. The woman seeks her lost coin throughout the house, searching for it even in the dirt. When she has found it, she calls her friends, saying: "Rejoice with me; for I have found the piece which I had lost." Lastly, the Lord adds the parable of the Prodigal Son. Practically the Lord says: "There you have My doctrine. I came to seek and to save the lost."

If you take a survey of the entire life of Jesus, you behold Him going about, not like a proud philosopher, not like a moralist, surrounded by champions of virtuous endeavor, whom He teaches how to attain the highest degree of philosophic perfection. No, he goes about seeking lost sinners and does not hesitate to tell the proud Pharisees that harlots and publicans will enter the kingdom of heaven rather than they. Thus He shows us quite plainly what His Gospel really is.

In various places in their confessions the papists explain that many laws were uttered by Christ of which Moses knew nothing; for instance, the law to love our enemies, the law not to seek private revenge, the law not to demand back what has been taken from us, etc. All these matters the papists declare to be "new laws." This is wrong; for even Moses has said: "You shall love the Lord God with all your heart and with all your soul and with all your might" (Deut. 6:5) and: "You shall love your neighbor as yourself" (Lev. 19:18). Now, Christ did not abrogate this law of Moses, but neither did He publish any new laws. He only opened up the spiritual meaning of the Law. Accordingly, He says in Matt. 5:17: "Think not that I have come to destroy the Law and the prophets; I have come not to abolish them, but to fulfill them." That means that He did not come to issue new laws, but to fulfill the Law for us, so that we may share His fulfillment.

Thesis VI

In the second place, the Word of God is not rightly divided when the Law is not preached in its full sternness and the Gospel not in its full sweetness, when, on the contrary, Gospel elements are mingled with the Law and Law elements with the Gospel.

The commingling of both doctrines occurs when Gospel elements are mingled with the Law, and *vice versa*. Let us investigate what Scripture says regarding this matter. To begin with, what does it say concerning the Law? How does it show us that we must not mingle any evangelical ingredient into the Law?

Gal. 3:11-12: A person becomes righteous in the sight of God solely by faith. The Law cannot make any person righteous because it has not a word to say about justifying and saving faith. That information is found only in the Gospel. The Law has nothing to say about grace.

Rom. 4:16: Faith is demanded of us, not in order that there might be at least some little work that we are to do, as otherwise there would be no difference between those who go to hell and those who go to heaven. No; righteousness is of faith in order that it may be of grace. Both statements are identical. When I say: "A person becomes righteous in the sight of God by faith," I mean to say: "He becomes righteous gratuitously, by grace, by God's making righteousness a gift to him." Nothing is demanded of the person; he is only told: "Stretch out your hand, and you have it." Just that is what faith is—reaching out the hand. Suppose a person had never heard a word concerning faith and, on being told the Gospel, would rejoice, accept it, put his confidence in it, and draw comfort from it, that person would have the true, genuine faith, although he may not have heard a word concerning faith.

No Gospel element, then, must be mingled with the Law. Anyone expounding the Law shamefully perverts it by injecting into it grace, the grace, loving-kindness, and patience of God, who forgives sin. A preacher must proclaim the Law in such a manner that there remains in it nothing pleasant to lost and condemned sinners. Every sweet ingredient injected into the Law is poison; it renders this heavenly medicine ineffective.

Matt. 5:17-19: When preaching the Law, you must ever bear in mind that the Law makes no concessions. That is utterly beside the character of the Law; it only makes demands. The Law says: "You must do this; if you fail to do it, you have no recourse to the patience, loving-kindness, and long-suffering of God; you will have to go to perdition for your wrongdoing." To make this point quite plain to us, the Lord says: "Whoever then relaxes one of the least of these commandments and teaches men so, shall be called least in the kingdom of heaven." That does not mean he shall have the lowest place assigned him in heaven, but he does not belong in the kingdom of heaven at all.

Gal. 3:10: If you would direct men to do good works and for their comfort add a remark like this: "You should, indeed, be perfect; however, God does not demand the impossible from us. Do what you can in your weakness; only be sincere in your intention!"—if you would speak thus, you would be preaching a damnable doctrine; for that is a shameful corruption of the Law. God never spoke like that from Sinai.

Rom. 7:14: When a minister preaches the Law, he must by all means bear in mind that the Law is spiritual; it works on the spirit, not on some member of the body; it is directed to the spirit in man, to his will, heart, and affections. That is the way it operates in every instance.

A proper preaching of the Law must measure up to these requirements: There is to be no ranting about abominable vices that may be rampant in the congregation. Continual ranting will prove useless. People may quit the practices that have been reproved, but in two weeks they will have relapsed into their old ways. You must, indeed, testify with great earnestness against transgressions of God's commandments, but you must also tell the people: "Even if you were to quit your habitual cursing, swearing, and the like, that would not make you Christians. You might go to perdition for all that. God is concerned about the attitude of your heart."

Rom. 3:20: God does not tell you to preach the Law in order thereby to make men godly. The Law makes no one godly; but when it begins to produce its proper effects, the person who is feeling its power begins to fume and rage against God.

By the spectacle of Sinai God has indicated to us how we are to preach the Law. True, we cannot reproduce the thunder and lightning of that day, except in a spiritual way. If we do, it will be a salutary sermon. There may be many in the audience who will say to themselves, "If that man is right, I am lost."

Some, indeed, may say: "That is not the way for an evangelical minister to preach." But it certainly is; he could not be an evangelical preacher if he did not preach the Law thus. The Law must precede the preaching of the Gospel, otherwise the latter will have no effect. First comes Moses, then Christ; or: First John the Baptist, the forerunner, then Christ. At first the people will exclaim, How terrible is all this! But presently the preacher passes over to the Gospel, and then the people are cheered. They see the object of the preacher's preceding remarks: he wanted to make them see how awfully contaminated with sins they were and how sorely they needed the Gospel.

Thesis VII

In the third place, the Word of God is not rightly divided when the Gospel is preached first and then the Law; sanctification first and then justification; faith first and then repentance; good works first and then grace.

A wrong division of the Word of God occurs when the various doctrines are not presented in their order; when something that should come last is placed first. Four types of this perverse sequence are possible.

In the first place, the order may be distorted if you preach the Gospel prior to the Law.

Mark 1:15: "Repent" is plainly a Law utterance. In the preaching of our Lord this comes first, being followed by the Gospel summons: "Believe in the Gospel."

Acts 20:21: The apostle preached repentance first and then faith; the Law first and then the Gospel.

Our Lord said *repentance and forgiveness of sins should be preached in His name among all nations, beginning from Jerusalem.* The Lord does not reverse the divine order, thus: "Forgiveness of sins and repentance."

The second perversion of the true sequence occurs when sanctification of life is preached before justification, the preaching of forgiveness of sins; for justification by grace is nothing else than forgiveness of sins. I become righteous by appropriating the righteousness of Christ as my own.

Ps. 130:4: The psalmist practically says to God: "First You must grant us forgiveness of sins; after that we shall begin to reverence You by walking in a new, sanctified life."

Ps. 119:32: First come the consolations of God, justification, the granting of pardon to the sinner, the forgiveness of sins. After that the psalmist expects to "run in the way of God's commandments."

1 Cor. 1:30: The first requisite is to obtain wisdom, knowledge of the way of salvation. This is the primary step. Next comes righteous-

ness, which we obtain by faith. Not until this has been attained comes sanctification. I must first know that God has forgiven my sins before it affords me real joy to lead a sanctified life. Before that it was a grievous burden to me. At first I was angry with God; I hated Him for demanding so many things of me. I should have liked to cast Him from His throne. I mused in my heart, it would be better if there were no God. But when I had been pardoned and justified, I delighted, not only in the Gospel but also in the Law.

John 15:5: The Savior desires that we be grafted in Him like branches in a vine. This means that we believe in Him with our whole heart, put our confidence and trust in Him, and embrace Him wholly with the arms of faith, so that we live only in Him, our Jesus, who has rescued us and saves us. When this takes place, we shall bear fruit. The Savior, then, shows that we must be justified before we can lead a sanctified life. If we become loose, severed branches, we wither and bear no fruit.

To confound justification and sanctification is one of the most horrid errors. Only by a strict separation of justification and sanctification is a sinner made to understand clearly and become certain that he has been received into grace by God; and this knowledge equips him with strength to walk in a new life.

The third perversion of the true sequence — first Law, then Gospel — occurs when faith is preached first and repentance next. If you wish to believe in Christ, you must become sick; for Christ is a physician only for those who are sick. He came to seek and to save the lost; therefore you must first become a lost and condemned sinner. He is the Good Shepherd, who goes in search of the lost sheep; therefore you must first realize that you are a lost sheep.

Finally, the fourth perversion occurs when good works are preached first and then grace.

Eph. 2:8-10: The apostle does not say: "We must do good works in order to have a gracious God," but the very opposite. When you have received grace, God has created you anew. In this new state you have to do good works; you can no longer remain under the dominion of sin.

Titus 2:11-12: Grace is brought to us first, and then this grace begins a work of education upon us. We are placed under the divine pedagogy of grace. The moment a person accepts the grace which brought God down from heaven that grace begins to train him. The object of this training is to teach him how to do good works and lead an upright life.

Romans contains the Christian doctrine in its entirety. In the first three chapters we find the sharpest preaching of the Law. This is followed, towards the end of the third chapter and in chapters 4 and 5, by the doctrine of justification — nothing but that. Beginning at chapter 6, the apostle treats of nothing else than sanctification. Here we have a true pattern of the correct sequence: first the Law, threatening men with the wrath of God; next the Gospel, announcing the comforting promises of God. This is followed by instruction regarding the things we are to do after we have become new men. The prophets, too, when they wished to convert people, began by preaching the Law to them. When the chastisings of the Law had taken effect, they comforted the poor sinners. As to the apostles, no sooner had their hearers shown that they were alarmed than they seemed to know nothing else to do for them than to comfort them and pronounce absolution to them. Not until that had been done would they say to their people: "Now you must show your gratitude toward God." They did not issue orders; they did not threaten when their orders were disregarded, but they pleaded and besought their hearers by the mercy of God to act like Christians.

That is genuine sanctification which follows upon justification; that is genuine justification which comes after repentance.

Thesis VIII

In the fourth place, the Word of God is not rightly divided when the Law is preached to those who are already in terror on account of their sins or the Gospel to those who live securely in their sins.

1 Tim. 1:8-10 and Is. 61:1-3 show us that according to God's Word not a drop of evangelical consolation is to be brought to those who are still living securely in their sins. On the other hand, to the brokenhearted not a syllable containing a threat or a rebuke is to be addressed, but only promises conveying consolation and grace, forgiveness of sin and righteousness, life and salvation.

That was the practice of our Lord. He was approached by a woman "who was a sinner" (Luke 7:37), who in the presence of self-righteous Pharisees knelt down, washed His feet with her hot tears, and dried them with her hair. She was crushed when she came to Jesus; there was no one to comfort her. But she turned to Jesus, for she had realized that where He was, there was the throne of grace. The Lord did not utter one word of reproof because of the sins she had committed—no, not a word. He simply said to her: "Your sins are forgiven." In another, a similar instance He dismissed the guilty woman with the assurance: "Neither do I condemn you," and with the brief admonition: "Go and do not sin again."

The Lord treated Zacchaeus the same way. He had gained the conviction that he could not go on in his sinful ways but must amend his conduct. When the Lord was about to pass in the neighborhood, he mounted a sycamore tree, because he wanted to see this holy man. The Lord, catching sight of him, called to him: "Zacchaeus, make haste and come down, for I must stay at your house today." Zacchaeus surely expected that the Lord would go over the record of his sins with him and hold up to him all the evil he had done. But Jesus did nothing of the kind. On the contrary, in the house of Zacchaeus He said: "Today salvation has come to this house, since he also is a son of Abraham." It is Zacchaeus who says: "Behold, Lord, the half of my goods I give to the poor; and if I have defrauded anyone of anything, I restore it fourfold." The Lord did not demand this of him, but his own conscience, first alarmed, but now quieted, demanded this joyful act of generosity to the poor from him.

The parable of the prodigal is another illustration. The Lord pictures him to us, after he had wasted everything he had, as returning to his father with a contrite heart. The father receives him without a word of censure and exclaims: "Let us eat and make merry; for this my son was dead and is alive again, he was lost and is found." A joyous banquet is prepared, but not a word of reproof is spoken.

This attitude the Lord maintains even on the cross. Next to Him hangs one who has led an infamous life. The patient suffering of Christ has given him a new understanding, which he voices in these words: "We, indeed, are justly in this condemnation; for we are receiving the due reward of our deeds; but this man has done nothing wrong." Turning finally to the Lord, he says: "Jesus, remember me when you come in Your kingly power." He recognizes in Jesus the Messiah. And now observe that the Lord does not reply, "What! You I am to remember? You, who have done so many wicked things?" No, He does not cast up his sins to him at all, but simply says: "Today you will be with Me in paradise."

By these incidents the Lord shows us what we are to do for a poor sinner who may have led a shameful life but has become crushed and contrite, full of terror because of his sins. In such a case we should not lose any time in censuring and reproving him, but absolve and comfort him. That is the way to divide the Gospel from the Law.

The practice of the apostles was identical with that of the Lord. Recall the incident of the jailer at Philippi. He was on the point of committing suicide when Paul called to him: "Do not harm yourself, for we are all here." All through the night he had heard Paul and Silas singing praises to God. No doubt a new knowledge had begun to dawn on him. When he heard Paul's warning cry, he came trembling and, falling down before Paul and Silas, said: "Men, what must I do to be saved?" They do not tell him of a number of things that he will have to do first, for instance, to feel contrite. They simply say to him: "Believe in the Lord Jesus, and you will be saved, you and your household." They simply invite him to accept the mercy of God; for that is what faith is — accepting the divine mercy, or grace.

The second part of the thesis tells us that the Word of God is not rightly divided if the Gospel is preached to such as live securely in their sins.

The latter error is as dangerous as the former. Incalculable damage

36

is done if the consolations of the Gospel are offered to secure sinners, or if one preaches to a multitude in such a manner that secure sinners imagine that the comfort of the Gospel is meant for them. The Gospel is not intended for secure sinners. We cannot, of course, prevent secure sinners from coming into our churches and hearing the Gospel, and it devolves upon the preacher to offer the entire comfort of the Gospel in all its sweetness, however in such a manner that secure sinners realize that the comfort is not intended for them. The whole manner of the preacher's presentation must make them realize that fact.

Matt. 7:6: What is meant by "what is holy"? Nothing else than the Word of Christ. What is meant by "pearls"? The consolation of the Gospel, with the grace, righteousness, and salvation it proclaims. Of these things we are not to speak to dogs, that is, to enemies of the Gospel; nor to swine, that is, to such as want to remain in their sins and are seeking their heaven and their bliss in the filth of their sins.

Is. 26:10: It is quite useless to offer mercy to the godless. They imagine either that they do not need it or that they already have all of it. The trifling sins, they say, of which they are guilty have long been forgiven. To a person of this stripe I am not to preach the Gospel; I am not to offer him mercy—for that is what preaching the Gospel means—because he will not be benefited by it. A wicked person, who wants to remain in his sins, "does not see the majesty of the Lord." He does not see what a great treasure is offered him. He does not understand the doctrine of salvation by grace; either he spurns it, or he shamefully misapplies it. He thinks: "If mere faith is all that is necessary for my salvation, my sins, too, are forgiven. I can remain such as I am, and I shall still go to heaven. I, too, believe in my Lord Jesus Christ."

A pattern after which we are to model our preaching we find, in the first place, in Christ. Observing His conduct, we find that whenever He met with secure sinners—and such the self-righteous Pharisees in those days certainly were—He had not a drop of comfort for them, but called them serpents and a vipers' brood, pronounced a tenfold woe against them, revealed their abominable hypocrisy, assigned them to perdition, and told them that they would not escape eternal damnation. Although He knew that these very persons would nail Him to the cross, He fearlessly told them the truth. That is a point to be noted by preachers. Though knowing in advance that they will share the fate of the Lord Jesus, they must preach the Law in all its severity to secure, reckless sinners, to hypocrites and men who are their enemies. Whenever the preacher faces this class of people, he dare not preach anything else than the Law to them. Moreover, when he preaches before a multitude, his hearers must get the impression that what he says does not apply to all of them indiscriminately, but to the would-be righteous who claim the Gospel for themselves.

True, our Lord says: "Come unto Me, *all*," but He immediately adds "who labor and are heavy laden." Thus He serves notice upon secure sinners that He is not inviting them.

On a certain occasion a rich young man approached Jesus and said to Him: "Good Teacher, what good thing must I do to have eternal life?" Christ declined the title and turned to the young man with the challenge: "Keep the commandments." When the young man asked, "Which?" Jesus said, "You shall not kill, you shall not commit adultery, you shall not steal, you shall not bear false witness, Honor your father and mother, and you shall love your neighbor as yourself." The young man replied: "All these I have observed from my youth; what do I still lack?" How does Christ answer the young man's last question? Does He say, "You lack faith"? By no means; since He is dealing with a miserable, secure and self-righteous person, He does not preach one word of Gospel to him. Jesus, accordingly, said: "If you would be perfect, go, sell what you possess, and give to the poor, and you will have treasure in heaven; and come, follow Me." Now the record states: "When the young man heard this, he went away sorrowful; for he had great possessions." He departed with an accusing conscience, which, no doubt, told him: "That is indeed a different doctrine from the one I used to hear. What He tells me I cannot do. I have become too greatly attached to my possessions. I would rather forfeit my fellowship with Him than do what He says. I am not going to roam the country with Him like a beggar." Probably his conscience also testified to him that according to the teaching of Christ he was damned, that hell was his goal. That was the effect which the Lord had intended to produce in dealing with this young man. In this episode we have an example to guide us when we are dealing with those who are still secure and self-righteous.

The apostles observed the same practice as their Lord. They first preached the Law, and with such force that their hearers were cut to the quick.

In his first Pentecostal sermon, Peter first fastened the murder of Christ upon his hearers, and that charge went home. They were frightened and asked: "Brethren, what shall we do?" Peter says: "Repent and be baptized, every one of you, in the name of Jesus Christ for the forgiveness of your sins." Preaching the Gospel to them, he tells them that they can have forgiveness of all their sins, even of the worst ones. That was the general practice of the apostles everywhere, not only in Jerusalem, but also in Athens, Corinth, Ephesus, etc. Everywhere they preached repentance first and then faith; for they knew that everywhere they were, as a rule, facing secure sinners who had not yet realized their most miserable, sinful condition. However, they did not only apply the Law sternly to those who had not yet heard anything about the Christian religion, but also to those who pretended to be Christians but were living securely in their sins.

There is a remarkable instance of their practice in the two concluding chapters of Second Corinthians. The holy apostle writes: "For I fear that perhaps I may come and find you not what I wish, and that you may find me not what you wish; that perhaps there may be quarreling, jealousy, anger, selfishness, slander, gossip, conceit, and disorder" (2 Cor. 12:20). He means to say: "You will imagine that I am going to preach the Gospel to you. But you will be surprised when I come and you will hear me preach." Among the things that he is going to preach he does not mention knavery, fornication, theft, blasphemy, murder, but all such sins, especially hypocrisy, as are still found in all Christian congregations. He proceeds, v. 21: "I fear that when I come again my God may humble me before you, and I may have to mourn over many of those who sinned before and have not repented of the impurity, immorality, and licentiousness which they have practiced." They were not at that time living in fornication and uncleanness, but they had formerly lived in these sins. They had become Christians by a process of reasoning, but had not truly repented of their sins. They professed the Christian religion with their lips, but their faith was not faith of the heart. They had not been regenerated and renewed by the Holy Spirit. Continuing, the apostle says: "This is the third time I am coming to you. Any charge must be sustained by the evidence of two or three witnesses. I warned those who sinned before and all the others, and I warn them now while absent, as I did when present on my second visit, that if I come again I will not spare them." (2 Cor. 13:1-2)

We have here an excellent example for a preacher to follow. When people begin to engage in all manner of sinful practices with impunity and imagine that everybody will have to regard them as good Christians provided they attend church and go to Communion, the pastor must say to himself: "It is time that I lay down the Law to my people, lest I live in careless ease while my hearers are going to perdition and lest they rise up to accuse me on the Last Day and say: You are the cause why we have to suffer eternal torment."

The apostle had to reflect that, when he resumed his ministry in the Corinthian congregation, he would still find secure members whom he would have to rouse. In those godless, sodomitical times the apostle did not care whether the people would turn against him and become his enemies. He told them in advance that he was not going to spare them. He would tell to their very faces that eternal damnation was awaiting them unless they would repent; he would rebuke them as being people who had been found out as continuing to sin against their conscience and yet claimed to be Christians.

Accordingly, we may not preach the Gospel, but must preach the Law to secure sinners. We must preach them into hell before we can preach them into heaven. By our preaching our hearers must be brought to the point of death before they can be restored to life by the Gospel. They must be made to realize that they are sick unto death before they can be restored to health by the Gospel. First their own righteousness must be laid bare to them, so that they may see of what filthy rags it consists, and then, by the preaching of the Gospel, they are to be robed in the garment of the righteousness of Christ. They must first be induced to say from the heart: "I, a lost and condemned creature" in order that they be induced, next, to exclaim joyfully: "Oh, blessed man that I am!" They must first be reduced to nothing by the Law in order that they may be made to be something, to the praise of the glory of God, by the Gospel.

Thesis IX

In the fifth place, the Word of God is not rightly divided when sinners who have been struck down and terrified by the Law are directed, not to the Word and the Sacraments, but to their own prayers and wrestlings with God in order that they may win their way into a state of grace; in other words, when they are told to keep on praying and struggling until they feel that God has received them into grace.

In order to obtain a divine assurance regarding the proper way of rightly dividing the Word, so as to meet the errors named in our thesis, let us examine a few pertinent examples recorded in Scripture. Let us observe the apostles, who divided the Word of God rightly and showed alarmed sinners the right way to rest and peace and assurance of their state of grace with God.

Acts 2: When these words of the apostle struck the hearts of the people, they "said to Peter and the rest of the apostles, Brethren, what shall we do?"

He said to them: "Repent and be baptized, every one of you, in the name of Jesus Christ for the forgiveness of your sins." Μετανοεῖτε ("repent") means: "Change your minds." It refers quite plainly to what is called the second part of repentance, viz., faith. The term is here used in the figure of synecdoche, because the Law had already done its work upon these hearers. Accordingly, it was far from the apostle Peter's mind to bring about their salvation by hurling them into still greater distress, anguish, and terror. Now that their heart had been pricked, he was satisfied. They were now prepared to hear the Gospel and receive it into their hearts. Therefore the apostle now addressed them: "You must change your minds and believe the Gospel of the Crucified One; you must dismiss all your errors and be baptized at once in the name of Jesus Christ for the forgiveness of sins."

Other demands the apostle did not make; his hearers were only to listen to his words and take comfort in these soothing words of consolation, this promise of the forgiveness of their sins, of life and salvation. We are not told about measures such as the sects in our day employ.

41

Acts 16: "And suddenly there was a great earthquake, so that the foundations of the prison were shaken; and immediately all the doors were opened, and everyone's fetters were unfastened. When the jailer woke and saw that the prison doors were open, he drew his sword and was about to kill himself, supposing that the prisoners had escaped" (vv. 26-27). If prisoners escaped from jail, the keeper of the prison was held responsible. In the case of especially dangerous characters the jailer was apt to be punished with death if they escaped. He calculated: Since I am to be sentenced to death anyway, what is life worth to me? I prefer to be my own executioner.

"But Paul cried with a loud voice, 'Do not harm yourself, for we are all here'" (v. 28). Imagine the impression that cry made on the jailer!

From the psalms the apostles had sung the jailer had very likely understood that they were men who wished to tell the people how to find a happy fate beyond Hades. In his great distress he now beseeches the apostles: "Men, what must I do to be saved?" (v. 30). If the apostles had been fanatics, they would have said to him: "My dear friend, this is no easy matter. Before a godless, reckless man like you can be saved, an elaborate and extensive cure is necessary, which we shall prescribe to you." Not a word of this. They behold in the jailer a person fit to receive the Gospel. He was as godless as before; he had not yet conceived a hatred of sin. He says nothing about that. All he wants is to escape the punishment of sin and obtain a happy, blessed fate beyond the grave.

That same night the jailer is converted, obtains faith and the assurance that he is accepted with God, and reconciled. He has become a beloved child of God.

What measures did the apostles apply to him? Nothing beyond proclaiming the Gospel to him without any condition attached to it. They tell him unqualifiedly: "Believe in the Lord Jesus." That makes the apostles' practice plain. In every instance where their word had produced faith, they administered Baptism immediately. They did not say: "We have to take you through an extensive course of instruction and expound to you accurately and thoroughly all the articles of the Christian creed. After that, we shall have to put you on probation to see whether you can become an approved Christian." Nothing of the sort. The jailer asks to be baptized because he knows that is the means for receiving him into the kingdom of Christ; and they promptly administer Baptism to him.

Acts 22: Ananias does not say to Paul: "First you must pray until you have a sensation of inward grace." No, he tells him: Having come to a knowledge of the Lord Jesus, your first step must be to receive Baptism for the washing away of your sins. And then call upon the Lord Jesus. That is the true order of saving grace: not praying first for the grace of God, but after one has learned to know the grace of God. Prior to that he cannot pray acceptably.

In this instance the practise of the Lord Himself is exhibited to us. He surely knows how to deal with poor sinners. As soon as Saul became alarmed about his sins, Jesus approached him with His consolation. He did not require him to experience all sorts of feelings, but promptly proclaimed to him the Word of Grace. That shows a true minister of Christ how to proceed when his object is to lead sinners who have been crushed by the Law to the assurance of the grace of God in Christ Jesus.

The method of the sects is the very contrary of this. True, they also preach the Law first with great sternness, which is quite proper. The only wrong feature in this part of their preaching is their depiction of the infernal torments, which is usually done in such a drastic manner as to engage the imagination rather than to make their words sink into the depth of the heart. They frequently preach excellent sermons on the Law with its awful threatenings; only they do not bring out its spiritual meaning. Instead of reducing their hearers to the condition where they profess themselves poor, lost, and condemned sinners, who have deserved everlasting wrath, they put them in a state of mind which makes them say: "Is it not terrible to hear God uttering such awful threatenings on account of sin?" If you do not lead a man by the Law to the point where he puts off completely the garment of his own righteousness and declares himself a miserable, wicked man, whose heart is sinning day and night with his evil lusts, thoughts, desires, dispositions, and wishes of all kinds, you have not preached the Law aright. A preacher of the Law must make a person distrust himself even in the least matter until his dying hour and keep him confessing that he is a miserable creature, with no record of good deeds except those which God has accomplished through him. If the heart is not put in such condition, the person is not properly prepared for the reception of the Gospel.

But the incorrect preaching of the Law is not the worst feature of the sects. They do not preach the Gospel to such as are alarmed and in anguish. They imagine they would commit the worst sin by immediately offering consolation to such poor souls. They give them a long list of efforts that they must make in order, if possible, to be received into grace: how long they must pray, how strenuously they must fight and wrestle and cry, until they can say that they feel they have received the Holy Ghost and divine grace and can rise from their knees shouting hallelujahs.

But the required feeling may rest on a false foundation. It may not be the testimony of the Holy Spirit in the heart, but a physical effect, produced by the lively presentations of the preacher. That explains why sincere persons who have become believers not infrequently feel one moment that they have found the Lord Jesus, and in the next, that they have lost Him again. Now they imagine that they are in a state of grace; at another time, that they are fallen from grace.

This faulty practice is based on three awful errors.

In the first place, the sects neither believe nor teach a real and complete reconciliation of man with God because they regard our heavenly Father as being a God very hard to deal with, whose heart must be softened by passionate cries and bitter tears. That amounts to a denial of Jesus Christ, who has long ago turned the heart of God to men by reconciling the entire world with Him. God does nothing by halves. In Christ He loves all sinners without exception. The sins of every sinner are canceled. Every debt has been liquidated. There is no longer anything that a poor sinner has to fear when he approaches his heavenly Father, with whom he has been reconciled by Christ.

However, people imagine that, after Christ has done His share, man must still do his, and man is not reconciled to God until both efforts meet. The sects picture reconciliation as consisting in this, that the Savior made God *willing* to save men, provided men would be willing on their part to be reconciled. But that is the reverse of the Gospel. God *is* reconciled. Accordingly, the apostle Paul calls on us: "Be reconciled to God." That means: Since God has been reconciled to you by Jesus Christ, grasp the hand which the Father in heaven holds out to you. Moreover, the apostle declares: "One has died for all; therefore all have died" (2 Cor. 5:14). That means: Christ died for the sins of all men, and this is tantamount to all men's dying and making satisfaction for their sins. Therefore nothing at all is required on the part of man to reconcile God; He already is reconciled. Righteousness lies ready; it must not first be achieved by man. If man were to attempt to do so, that would be an awful crime, a battle against grace and against the reconciliation and perfect redemption accomplished by the Son of God.

In the second place, the sects teach false doctrine concerning the Gospel. They regard it as nothing else than an instruction for man, teaching him what he must do to secure the grace of God, while in reality the Gospel is God's proclamation to men: "You are redeemed from your sins; you are reconciled to God; your sins are forgiven."

In the third place, the sects teach false doctrine concerning faith. They regard it as a quality in man by which he is improved. For that reason they consider faith such an extraordinarily important and salutary matter.

It is true, indeed, that genuine faith changes a person completely. It brings love into a person's heart. Faith cannot be without love, just as little as fire can be without heat. But this quality of faith is not the reason why it justifies us, giving us what Christ has acquired for us, what hence is ours already and only need be received by us. The Scriptural answer to the question: "What must I do to be saved?" is: "You must believe; hence you are not to do anything at all yourself." In that sense the apostle answered the question when it was addressed to him. He practically told the jailer: "You are to do nothing but accept what God has done for you, and you have it and become a blessed person."

No doctrine of the Evangelical Lutheran Church is more offensive to the Reformed than the doctrine that the grace of God, the forgiveness of sins, righteousness in the sight of God, and eternal salvation, is obtained in no other way than by the believer's putting his confidence in the written Word, in Baptism, in the Lord's Supper, and in absolution. The Reformed declare that this way of getting into heaven is too mechanical, and on hearing the Lutheran teaching they denounce it. They say: "What does baptizing with earthly water profit? The true baptism is baptizing with the Spirit and with fire." Again: "What is the benefit of eating and drinking the natural body and blood of Christ? The true food and drink by which the hunger and thirst of the soul is really stilled is the truth that came down from heaven." Finally, they say: "How can I be helped by a mortal, sinful man, who cannot look into my heart, saying to me: 'Your sins are forgiven you'? No; my sins are not forgiven except when God Himself speaks these words in my heart and makes me feel their force."

According to the Holy Scriptures, Baptism is not a mere washing with earthly water, but the Spirit of God, yea, Jesus with His blood, connects with it for the purpose of cleansing me of my sins. Therefore Ananias says to Saul: "Be baptized and wash away your sins" (Acts 22:16); and Jesus says to Nicodemus: "Truly, truly, I say to you, unless one is born of water and the Spirit, he cannot enter the kingdom of God" (John 3:5). He names the water first and then the Spirit, for it is by this very baptizing with water that the Spirit is to be given me. In Gal. 3:27 the apostle says clearly and distinctly: "As many of you as were baptized into Christ have put on Christ"; and in Titus 3:5-7: "He saved us, not because of deeds done by us in righteousness, but in virtue of His own mercy, by the washing of regeneration and renewal in the Holy Spirit, which He poured out upon us richly through Jesus Christ our Savior, so that we might be justified by His grace and become heirs in hope of eternal life."

According to the Holy Scriptures the Lord's Supper is not an earthly feast, but a heavenly feast on earth, in which not only bread and wine, or only the body and blood of Christ are given us, but together with these forgiveness of sins, life, and salvation is given and sealed to us. For, distributing the bread which He had blessed, Christ said: "This is My body, which is given *for you*. Do this in remembrance of Me." By the words "for you" He invited the disciples to ponder the fact that they were now receiving and eating that body by the bitter death of which on the cross the entire world would be redeemed. He meant to remind them that they ought to break forth with joy and gladness because the ransom that was to be paid for the sins of the whole world was, so to speak, put in their mouths. Offering the disciples the cup which He had blessed, Christ said: "This cup is the new testament in My blood, which is shed for you." Why did He add the words "shed for you"? He meant to say: "When receiving the blood of redemption in this Holy Supper, you receive at the same time what has been acquired on the cross by means of this sacrifice."

Finally, according to the Holy Scriptures the absolution pronounced by a poor, sinful preacher is not his absolution, but the absolution of Jesus Christ Himself; for the preacher absolves a person by the command of Christ, in the place of Christ, in the name of Christ. Christ said to His disciples: "As the Father has sent Me, even so I send you" (John 20:21). What is the import of these words? None other than this: "I have been sent by My Father. When I speak to you, My words are the words of My Father. You must not consider the humble form in which you see Me. I come in the name of the Father, in the place of the Father, and the word of promise that proceeds from My mouth is the word of My Father. Now, in the same manner as My Father has sent Me I am sending you. You, too, are to speak in My name, in My place." Therefore He continues: "Receive the Holy Spirit. If you forgive the sins of any, they are forgiven; if you retain the sins of any, they are retained."

The Spirit comes to men by means of the Word. A person may

imagine that he is full of the Spirit to the bursting point, but it is his own spirit of fanaticism. The true Spirit is obtained only through the Word of God. In every passage of the Holy Scriptures which recounts the conversion of people we see that God wants to deal with men only through the Word and Sacraments.

To a hearing person I can preach the Gospel by words. In the case of a deaf person, whom I cannot teach by that method, I may take a picture representing the birth of Christ with the angels coming out of heaven or one that represents the crucifixion. By way of pantomime I can explain the pictures and instruct the deaf without speaking a word to him. That is what God does by means of the sacraments, which show us in a picture, so to speak, what God proclaims audibly in the Word. "The sacraments are the visible Word," that is an excellent axiomatic utterance of Augustine. A person, therefore, who speaks of the sacraments with depreciation and contempt says the same things against the Word. He redicules God, turning Him into a wretched master of ceremonies, who has prescribed all sorts of pantomimes for us merely for the purpose of exercising our faith.

The Protestant churches, so called, which are outside of the pale of the Evangelical Lutheran Church, know nothing of the true way to forgiveness of sin by means of the Word and, in general, through the means of grace. This is evident, in particular, from their rejection of absolution as pronounced by the minister in general and private confession. These so-called Protestant churches assert that of all Protestant churches the Lutheran has really been reformed least; for, they say, it still retains much of the leaven of the Romish Church, the worst being absolution.

Our doctrine is entirely different: "The Office of the Keys is the *peculiar church power* which Christ has given to His *church* on earth, to forgive the sins of penitent sinners unto them and to retain the sins of the impenitent so long as they do not repent." Mark this phrase: "peculiar church power"! It means that the power has been given, not to the preachers, but to the church. The preachers are not the church, but only servants of the church. They are joint owners with others of the Office of the Keys; however, the keys do not belong to the preachers exclusively, but to the church, to every individual member of the church. The humblest day-laborer possesses them just as well as the most highly esteemed general superintendent. The Lutheran practice of absolution rests on the following facts:

1. Christ, the Son of God, took upon Himself by imputation all sins of every sinner, counting them as His own. Accordingly, John the

Baptist, pointing to Christ, says: "Behold the Lamb of God, who takes away the sin of the world!" (John 1:29)

2. By His life in poverty, by His suffering, crucifixion, and death, Christ has wiped out the record of the world's sin and procured remission of all sins. No man living, from Adam to the last human being that will be born, is excepted from this plan.

3. By raising His Son Jesus Christ from the dead, God the Father confirmed, and put the stamp of approval on, the work of reconciliation and redemption which Christ finished on the cross. For by the resurrection of Christ He has declared: "As My Son has cried on the cross, 'It is finished,' so I announce, It is finished indeed! You sinners are redeemed. Forgiveness of sins is prepared for everybody; it is ready; it must not first be acquired by you."

4. By His command to preach the Gospel to every creature, Christ commanded at the same time to preach forgiveness of sins to all men, hence to bring to them the glad tidings: "All that is necessary for your salvation has been accomplished. When asking, What must we do to be saved? just remember that all has been done. There is nothing more to do. You are only to believe all that has been done for you, and you will be relieved."

5. Christ did not only issue a general command to His apostles and their successors in office to preach the Gospel, hence the forgiveness of sin, but to minister to each individual who desires it this comfort: "You are reconciled to God." For if forgiveness of sins has been procured for all, it has been procured for each individual. If I may offer it to all, I may offer it to each individual. Not only *may* I do this, I am *ordered* to do it. If I fail to do it, I am a servant of Moses and not a servant of Christ.

6. Now that forgiveness of sin has been procured not only has a minister a special commission to proclaim it, but every Christian, male or female, adult or child, is commissioned to do this. Even a child's absolution is just as certain as the absolution of St. Peter, yea, as the absolution of Christ would be, were He again to stand visibly before men and say: "Your sins are forgiven you." There is no difference; it is not a question of what man must do, but what has been done by Christ.

The removal of sins is not based on a mysterious power of the pastor, but on the fact that Christ has taken away the sins of the world long ago and that everybody is to tell this fact to his fellowmen. This is the duty, naturally, especially of preachers, not, however, because of a peculiar power inherent in them, but because God has ordained their office for the administration of the means of grace, the Word and the sacraments. In an emergency it becomes evident that a layman has the authority to do what a prelate or a superintendent does, and to do it just as effectually.

Contrition is necessary, but not as a means for acquiring forgiveness of sins. If I am a proud Pharisee, what do I care for the forgiveness of sins? I shall be like the surfeited glutton who turns up the nose at the finest food and drink that is set before him.

Let us not misunderstand Luther. He did not proclaim the consolations of the Gospel to sinners living in carnal security; he gave them no comfort. But when a person was contrite and longed for forgiveness of sins, he would say to him: Here it is; take it, and you have it.

Luther is right also in advising men not to inquire at all about the quality and sufficiency of their contrition. For any person to build his hope on that means to build it on sand. On the contrary, a person is to praise God for the absolution he has received; that makes his contrition salutary. The right procedure is not to base the validity of absolution on our own contrition, but to make our contrition rest on our absolution.

Luther insists on faith in the declaration of Christ: "Your sins are forgiven you." To disbelieve this statement is tantamount to making Christ a liar. Though a minister pronounce the absolution to such a person ten times, it would not benefit him. We cannot look into people's hearts; but that is not necessary at all; we are to look only in the Word of our heavenly Father, which informs us that God has absolved the entire world. That assures us that all sins have been forgiven to all men.

Does this apply also to an impious scoundrel, who may be plotting burglary tonight, with the object of stealing and robbing? Indeed it does. The reason why he is not benefited by absolution is because he does not accept the forgiveness offered him; for he does not believe in his absolution. If he believed the Holy Spirit, he would quit stealing.

Is it right to absolve a scoundrel of this kind? If he is known to you as a scoundrel, it is wrong because you know that he will not accept forgiveness. Knowing this, you would commit a great and grievous sin by performing the sacred act of absolution for him. But absolution itself is always valid. If Judas had received absolution, his sins would have been forgiven by God; but he would have had to accept forgiveness. To obtain this treasure, there must be one who bestows it, and another who receives it. An unbeliever may imagine and even say that he accepts forgiveness, but in his heart he is resolved to continue his sinful life and to prefer serving the devil. Hence the true doctrine of absolution does not make men secure, but thoroughly and radically plucks them out of the devil's kingdom.

The last part of Thesis IX tells us in particular that the Word of God is not rightly divided "when sinners who have been struck down and terrified by the Law are directed . . . to their own prayers and wrestlings with God in order that they may win their way into a state of grace; in other words, when they are told to keep on praying and struggling *until they feel* that God has received them into grace."

There are people who regard themselves as good Christians although they are spiritually dead. They have never felt a real anguish on account of their sins; they have never been filled with terror on account of them, have never been appalled by the thought of the hell which they have deserved, have never been on their knees before God, bewailing with bitter tears their awful, damnable condition under sin. Much less have they wept sweet tears of joy and glorified God for His mercy. They read and hear the Word of God without being specially impressed by it. They go to church and receive absolution without feeling refreshed; they attend Holy Communion without any inward sensation and remain as cold as ice. Occasionally, when they become inwardly agitated because of their indifference in matters concerning their salvation and because of their lack of appreciation of God's Word, they try to quiet their heart with the reflection that the Lutheran Church teaches that the lack of spiritual feeling is of no moment. They reason that this lack cannot harm them and that they can be good Christians notwithstanding, because they consider themselves believers.

However, they labor under a grievous self-delusion. People in that condition have nothing but the dead faith of the intellect, a specious faith, or, to express it still more drastically, a lip faith. They may say with their mouths, "I believe," but their heart is not conscious of it. No, indeed; a person who cannot say, in accordance with Ps. 34:8, that he has *tasted* and seen that the Lord is good must not regard himself as being in a state of true faith. Moreover, the apostle Paul says (Rom. 8:16): "The Spirit Himself bears witness with our spirit that we are the children of God." Can the Holy Spirit bear this witness in us without our feeling it? The witness in court must speak loud enough for the judge to hear. The same is necessary in this case. According to God's Word any person who has never felt the testimony of the Spirit that he is the child of God is spiritually dead. He can offer no testimony in his favor and does wrong by considering himself a Christian nevertheless.

Rom. 5:1: Objective peace, established through the shedding of Christ's blood, exists prior to our justification. Accordingly, the apostle must be speaking of a peace that is sensed, felt, and experienced.

Rom. 14:17: The joy of which the apostle speaks is not worldly or carnal joy, but spiritual joy. A person that has tasted all the other joys except the last, is spiritually dead.

The examples of the saints corroborate this point. We behold them continually aglow with the praise of God because of what He has done for them. That presupposes that their hearts were conscious of the mercy which the Lord had shown them. Could David, without an inward experience, have exclaimed: "Bless the Lord, O my soul; and all that is within me, bless His holy name! Bless the Lord, O my soul, and forget not all His benefits who forgives all your iniquity, who heals all your diseases"?

Lastly, ask any person who has all the criteria of a true, living Christian whether he has experienced all the things of which he speaks, and he will answer in the affirmative. He will tell you that his heart is melting within him at every remembrance of his Savior's love. Again, he will also tell you that, in spite of the fact that he knows he has obtained grace, he is frequently seized with fright and anguish at the sight of the Law.

Law and Gospel are grievously commingled by those who assert that assurance of the forgiveness of sins requires praying, struggling, and wrestling until finally a joyful feeling arises in the heart, indicating to the person in a mysterious way that grace is now in his heart and that he can be of good cheer because he has forgiveness of his sins. Now, properly speaking, grace is never in man's, but in God's heart. *First* a person must *believe; after that he may feel.* Feeling proceeds from faith, not faith from feeling. If a person's faith proceeds from feeling, it is not genuine faith; for faith requires a divine promise which it lays hold of. Accordingly, we can be sure that the faith of those who can say: "I regard nothing in all the world except the precious Gospel; on that I build," is of the right sort.

1 John 3:19-20: A Christian may feel the accusation of his own heart, and when trying to quiet his heart he may hear a voice telling him that he is damned, that he has no forgiveness of his sins and no grace, is not a child of God and cannot hope for life eternal. To such a person the apostle says: "If our heart condemns us, God is greater than our heart." That is to say, our heart is indeed a judge, yet only a

subordinate one. A higher judge, namely God, is above our heart. I can say to my troubled heart: "Be still, my heart! Keep silence, my conscience! I have appealed to a higher court and inquired of God, the supreme Judge, whether I am rid of my sins. From the higher court, which can always reverse the verdict of a lower court, I have obtained a verdict that my sins are forgiven, for I cling to the Word of God." A person who by the grace of God is enabled to believe this is a blessed person. Though all the devils in hell roar at him, "You are lost!" he can answer them: "It is not so; I am not lost, but redeemed forever. Here I have the written evidence in God's Word." And in due time the feeling of grace will return. In the very moment when a Christian imagines that he is void of all feeling, cold, and dead, a miserable, lost creature, to whom the Word of God tastes like rotten wood, who does not relish absolution and has not the witness of the Holy Spirit in him, and all is over with him — just in such a moment a great joy may suddenly enter his heart. God will not leave him in the slough of despair.

True, we cannot lay down rules for God. There is a great difference among Christians. Some have been highly favored in being led an easy way by God, always enjoying a beautiful, pleasant feeling and never being in need of strong wrestling. For persons who always find their experiences in harmony with the Word of God need not struggle for that harmony. Others, however, are nearly always led by God through darkness, great anguish, grievous doubts, and diverse afflictions. In the latter case we must be careful to distinguish between one who is dead and one who is afflicted. The distinction is not difficult. If I am worried about my lack of the feeling of grace for which I am earnestly longing, that is proof that I am a true Christian. For one who desires to believe *is* already a believer. For how could a person possibly desire to believe something which he regards untrue? No man desires to be deceived. As soon as I want to believe something, I am secretly believing it.

John 20:29: The Lord's remarks to Thomas mean that we must *first* believe and *then* see and must not desire first to see and then to believe. It is certain, then, that we must not desire first to *feel,* but we must rather believe and then wait until God grants us the sweet sensation that our sins have been taken from us.

Heb. 11:1: If faith is what is here stated: a firm, reliant confidence, not doubting, not wavering, it is self-evident that faith dare not be based on sight, feeling, and sense. If it is, it is built on sand, and the entire structure thus set up will soon collapse.

The sects all have this grievous error in common, that they do not rely solely on Christ and His Word, but chiefly on something that takes place in themselves. As a rule, they imagine that all is well with them because they have turned from their former ways. As if that were a guarantee of reaching heaven! No; we are not to look back to our conversion for assurance, but we must go to our Savior again and again, every day, as though we never had been converted. My former conversion will be of no benefit to me if I become secure. I must return to the mercy-seat every day, otherwise I shall make my former conversion my savior, by relying on it. That would be awful; for in the last analysis it would mean that I make myself my savior.

Thesis X

In the sixth place, the Word of God is not rightly divided when the preacher describes faith in a manner as if the mere inert acceptance of truths, even while a person is living in mortal sins, renders that person righteous in the sight of God and saves him; or as if faith makes a person righteous and saves him for the reason that it produces in him love and reformation of his mode of living.

Luther taught that those who would be saved must have a faith *that produces love spontaneously and is fruitful in good works.* That does not mean that faith saves on account of the love which springs from it, but that the faith which the Holy Spirit creates and which cannot but do good works justifies because it clings to the gracious promises of Christ and because it lays hold of Christ. It is active in good works because it is genuine faith. The believer need not at all be exhorted to do good works; his faith does them automatically. The believer engages in good works, not from a sense of duty, in return for the forgiveness of his sins, but chiefly because he cannot help doing them. It is altogether impossible that genuine faith should not break forth from the believer's heart in works of love.

Gal. 5:6: The ineffectiveness of a faith that fails to work by love is not due to a lack of love, but to the fact that it is not real, honest faith. Love must not be added to faith but grow out of it. A fruitful tree does not produce fruit by somebody's order, but because, while there is vitality in it and it is not dried up, it must produce fruit spontaneously. Faith is such a tree; it proves its vitality by bearing fruit.

Acts 15:9: A person who claims to have a firm faith which he will never abandon, but who still has an impure heart, must be told that he is in great darkness; for he has no faith at all. You may regard all the doctrines that are preached in the Lutheran Church as true, but if your heart is still in its old condition, filled with the love of sin, if you still act contrary to your conscience, your whole faith is mere sham. Yours is not the faith of which the Holy Spirit speaks when He uses the word "faith" in the Scriptures; for that faith—the genuine article—purifies the heart.

John 5:44: An awful verdict is pronounced in these words by the Savior on those who seek honor from men: they have no faith. It is one of the fruits of faith that from the moment it begins to grow up in the heart it gives all honor to God alone.

We are all haughty, proud, and ambitious, and this noxious vice can be driven from our hearts only by the Holy Ghost. But we never become rid of it entirely; an evil root remains in the heart. A believer, when noticing this thing in himself, abominates it, reprobates himself, feels ashamed of himself, and asks God to deliver him from these abominable notions of pride.

The Savior's words are in the form of a rhetorical question and signify: You cannot believe, for seeking honor from men and believing are simply incompatible. The entrance of faith into the heart has the effect of making the believer humble in the presence of God and men.

James 2:1: Preferring the rich, because of their wealth, to the poor means respecting people's person, and that is something which faith will not tolerate. The believer views everyone not as far as his personality is concerned but in his relation to God. To him a poor beggar, having been redeemed by the blood of the Son of God, is worth as much as a king or an emperor.

Such are the miracles which faith works in our hearts.

Now, to represent justifying and saving faith as the inert mental act of regarding certain matters as true, which can coexist with mortal sin, means to treat faith as a work which man can produce in himself and preserve in himself even while sinning. True faith is a treasure which only the Holy Spirit can bestow.

Faith and good conscience must be companions. A person that has no good conscience certainly is without faith. Of such people the apostle says that they have "made shipwreck of their faith." (1 Tim. 1:19)

Even after our conversion we lack the true fear of God, and all our sins are great sins. Even the so-called sins of weakness of which the righteous cannot rid themselves must not be regarded as a paltry matter. Although they do not extinguish faith, they are no jest.

The second part of the tenth thesis states that the Word of God, the Law and the Gospel, is not rightly divided *when the preacher describes faith in a manner as if it makes a person righteous and saves him for the reason that it produces in him love and a reformation of his mode of living.*

The renewal of heart, love, and the good works which faith produces are not the justifying and saving element in a person's faith.

Rom. 4:16: The very reason why we teach righteousness by faith is because we teach that a person is justified in the sight of God and saved by grace. Now, if faith were to make us righteous because of some good quality inherent in us, it would be a wrong conclusion to teach a person's justification by faith, since he is justified and saved by grace. Justification is by grace, through faith; however, not because of good qualities inherent in faith. In justification that is not at all taken into consideration, but merely the fact that Jesus Christ has long ago redeemed the entire world, that He has done and suffered all that men ought to have done and suffered, and that men are merely to accept His work as their own. Hence the way to salvation is this: We are doing nothing, absolutely nothing, towards our salvation, but Christ has already done everything for us, and we must merely cling to what He has done, draw consolation from His finished work of redemption, and trust in it for our salvation. If something that we must do belonged to the justifying quality of faith, the apostle would in this text be drawing a false conclusion.

Phil. 3:8-9: The apostle declares that he is righteous; however, the righteousness which he has obtained by faith is not at all his own righteousness, but the righteousness of Christ. Accordingly, when we become righteous by faith, we are made righteous by an alien righteousness. God beholds in us absolutely nothing that He could count as righteousness to our credit. It is Another's righteousness which we have by faith. We have not acquired it or contributed anything towards it.

Rom. 4:5: Anyone possessing genuine faith acknowledges that he has been godless and that a divine miracle of grace was performed on him when God said to him the moment he believed in his Savior: "You are counted as righteous; I see in you no righteousness of your own, but I cover you with the righteousness of My Son and from now on see in you nothing but righteousness." Whoever does not come to Christ as an ungodly person does not come to Him at all.

Eph. 2:8-9: This sounds as if the apostle felt that he was not saying enough to keep men from being led astray into self-righteousness. First he says: "By grace are ye saved"; next, he adds: "through faith." Lest someone think he had achieved this feat by his faith, the apostle continues: "and that not of yourselves." Whence, then, is it? "It is the gift of God"; and to head off any thought of a person's own merit, he adds: "not of works," such as a person's love, or charity, would be. He winds up with the statement: "Lest any man should boast."

Rom. 11:6: The apostle tries to make the element of grace quite plain. He invites his readers to reflect that, when they admit that their salvation is "by grace," it cannot be by merit, for that would destroy the idea of grace. Adding merit to grace renders grace void. On the other hand, if salvation is by the merit of works, grace does not count, or merit would not be merit. Nothing remains, then, for a person but to believe firmly that he has been made righteous out of God's pure, everlasting mercy, by faith. Even when his faith bears good fruits, these follow later, after he has received all that is necessary for his salvation. First a person is saved, then he becomes godly. First he must be made an heir of heaven, then he becomes a different person.

That is why Luther says that the Christian religion is, in a word, a religion of gratitude. All the good that Christians do is not done to merit something. We would not know what to take up for the purpose of acquiring merit. Everything has been given us: righteousness, our everlasting heritage, our salvation. All that remains for us to do is to thank God. And then there is this, that out of great kindness God proposes to give to those who are specially faithful in this life a peculiar glory in addition to their salvation. That is no paltry affair in the life to come. For God bestows extraordinary gifts when He gives those gifts of glory. There will be a great difference among Christians in the life to come. For even the least plus which one of the saints receives above that which his fellow-saints get in heaven is no trifle.

The real good works, therefore, are works to which gratitude toward God prompts us. Whoever has true faith never thinks of meriting something good for himself by his service. He cannot help expressing his gratitude by love and good works. His heart has been changed; it has been softened by the richness of God's love which he has experienced. Over and above this God is so gracious that He rewards even the good works which He accomplishes in us. For the good works done by Christians are God's works.

Thesis XI

In the seventh place, the Word of God is not rightly divided when there is a disposition to offer the comfort of the Gospel only to those who have been made contrite by the Law, not from fear of the wrath and punishment of God, but from love of God.

Since the Fall the Law has but a single function, viz., to lead men to the knowledge of their sins. It has no power to renew them. That power is vested solely in the Gospel. Only faith works by love; we do not become spiritually active by love, by sorrow over our sins. On the contrary, while still ignorant of the fact that God has become our reconciled God and Father through Christ, we hate Him. An unconverted person who claims that he loves God is stating an untruth and is guilty of a miserable piece of hypocrisy, though he may not be conscious of it. He sets up a specious claim, because only faith in the Gospel regenerates a person. Accordingly, a person cannot love God while he is still without faith. To demand of a poor sinner that he must, from love of God, be alarmed on account of his sins and feel sorry for them is a perversion of Law and Gospel.

Here is the Biblical doctrine: The sinner is to come to Jesus just as he is, even when he has to acknowledge that there is nothing but hatred of God in his heart, and he knows of no refuge to which he may flee for salvation. A genuine preacher of the Gospel will show such a person how easy his salvation is: Knowing himself a lost and condemned sinner and unable to find the help that he is seeking, he must come to Jesus with his evil heart and his hatred of God and God's Law; and Jesus will receive him as he is. It is His glory that men say of Him: Jesus receives sinners. He is not to become a different being, he is not to become purified, he is not to amend his conduct, *before* coming to Jesus. He who alone is able to make him a better man is Jesus; and Jesus will do it for him if he will only believe.

Rom. 3:20: The Law produces, not love but the knowledge of sin. A person can, indeed, possess that knowledge without love of God.

Rom. 5:20: Many sins are slumbering in a person who is still ignorant of the Law. Let the Law be preached to such a person forcefully, let it strike his conscience with lightning force, and the person will not become better, but worse. He begins to rear up against God and say: "What! I am to be damned? True, I know that I am an enemy of God. But that is not my fault; I cannot help it." That is the effect of the preaching of the Law. It drives men to desperation. Blessed the person who has been brought to this point: he has taken a great step forward on the way to his salvation. Such a person will receive the Gospel with joy, while another, who has never passed through an experience of this kind, yawns when he hears the Gospel preached and says: "That is an easy way to get to heaven!" Only a poor sinner, on the brink of despair, realizes what a message of joy the Gospel is and joyfully receives it. See also Rom. 4:15; 7:7-8; Gal. 3:21; 2 Cor. 3:6.

These Bible texts are illustrated by examples recorded in Scripture, which exactly relate the conduct of certain persons before their conversion and after they had become believers.

On the first Christian festival of Pentecost a multitude of people had gathered and heard the apostle Peter preach. The gist of his remarks was that they were the murderers of the Messiah, Jesus of Nazareth, and must tremble when thinking of the Judgment. They had listened to Peter's whole address, but when he reached the point where he raised this charge against them, they became alarmed by the Holy Spirit. The record says: "They were cut to the heart." They reasoned: If we have done that, we are all doomed men. We are not told that they said: "Oh, we feel so sorry for having grieved our faithful God." It was not love of God, but fright and terror that made them cry: "What shall we do?" Nor does the apostle Peter say to them: "My dear people, we shall now have to investigate the quality of your contrition, whether it flows from love of God or from fear of the punishment due you for your sins, from fear of hell." The apostle says: "Repent and be baptized, every one of you, in the name of Jesus Christ for the forgiveness of your sins." We are told that they received Baptism immediately. Their change of mind consisted in this, that they no longer desired to be murderers of Jesus, but wished to believe in Him. Accordingly, the apostles received them, and they were numbered with the congregation of those who were saved.

The example of the jailer at Philippi also illustrates the point. When he imagined that all his prisoners had escaped during the earthquake, he was seized with despair and wanted to commit suicide. Paul cried to him: "Do not harm yourself, for we are all here"; and now the jailer fell writhing and trembling at the apostles' feet and asked: "Men, what must I do to be saved?" Nothing but his fright and terror moved him to do that. Now Paul does not say to him: "First you must become contrite from love of God," but: "Believe in the Lord Jesus, and you will be saved, you and your household."

Saul was put through the same experience. When the Gospel with its power had entered into his heart, this wretched man was plucked out of his distress and misery. And now the Lord prescribed for this sinner, who had been terrified and crushed and then comforted, no other lesson than this, that instead of persecuting Him, he was to confess Him after he had received Baptism as a seal of the forgiveness of his sins.

When you preach, do not be stingy with the Gospel; bring its consolations to all, even to the greatest sinners. When they are terrified by the wrath of God and hell, they are fully prepared to receive the Gospel. True, this goes against our reason; we think it strange that such knaves are to be comforted immediately; we imagine they ought to be made to suffer much greater agony in their conscience.

There is a passage in Scripture that is frequently misunderstood, namely 2 Cor. 7:10: *For godly sorrow worketh repentance to salvation not to be repented of; but the sorrow of the world worketh death.* "Godly sorrow" is supposed to mean sorrow of contrition from love of God. This is a mistake. The apostle refers to sorrow which man has not produced himself, but which God has caused in him by His Word. It is another grievous perversion of the Christian doctrine to tell an alarmed sinner that he must first experience contrition, and when he asks how he must go about that, to tell him that he must sit down and meditate and try to draw, or elicit, repentance from his heart. There is not in all the world a person who can produce contrition in himself. *Godly* sorrow is required because faith is required. God, by terrifying us, wants to produce this sorrow. We must not imagine that contrition is a good work which we do, but it is something that God works in us. God comes with the hammer of the Law and smites our soul. A person who wants to make himself sorrowful desires ever to increase his sorrow over sin. But a person merged in the right kind of sorrow yearns to be rid of it.

The Lutheran Confessions offer to poor sinners this sweet comfort, that, when God has given them the grace to be alarmed on account of their sins, they are in a fit condition to approach the throne of grace, where they receive forgiveness—the true remedy for their ills. They must indeed have contrition; however, not to the end of acquiring some merit by it, but that they may gladly accept what Jesus offers them.

When I am terrified by the thought of my sins, hell, death, and damnation and perceive that God is angry with me and that, being under His wrath, I am damned on account of my sins—that is godly sorrow, even though I may be in the same condition in which Luther was before he got the right knowledge of the Gospel. Such sorrow comes from God. On the other hand, when a fornicator, a rake, a drunkard, begins to sorrow because he has wasted the beautiful time of his youth, has ruined his body, and has become prematurely senile—that is a sorrow of this world. When a vain person is thrown into sorrow over his sins because he has lost somewhat of his prestige; when a thief sorrows over his thieving because it has landed him in jail—that is worldly sorrow. However, when a person grieves over his sins because he sees hell before him, where he will be punished for having insulted the most holy God, that is godly sorrow, provided that it has not been produced by imagination through a person's own effort. Genuine godly sorrow can be produced by God alone.

Thesis XII

In the eighth place, the Word of God is not rightly divided when the preacher represents contrition alongside of faith as a cause of the forgiveness of sin.

There is no question but that contrition is necessary if a person wishes to obtain forgiveness of his sins. At His first public exercise of the preaching function our Lord cried: "Repent and believe the Gospel." He names repentance first. Whenever this term is placed in opposition to faith, it signifies nothing else than contrition. When Christ gathered the apostles about Him for the last time, He said to them: "Thus it is written, that the Christ should suffer and on the third day rise from the dead, and that repentance and forgiveness of sins should be preached in His name" (Luke 24:46-47). Why is repentance required as well as faith? Our Lord gives the reason in these words: "Those who are well have no need of a physician, but those who are sick. . . . I came not to call the righteous, but sinners." (Matt. 9:12-13). With these words the Lord testifies that the reason why contrition is absolutely necessary is that without it no one is fit to be made a believer. He is surfeited and spurns the invitation to the heavenly marriage feast. As far back as Solomon we find this proverb: "He who is sated loathes honey." (Prov. 27:7). Where there is no spiritual hunger and thirst, the Lord Jesus is not received. As long as a person has not been reduced to the state of a poor, lost, and condemned sinner, he has no serious interest in the Savior of sinners.

However, contrition is not a cause of the forgiveness of sins. Contrition is not necessary on account of the forgiveness of sin, but on account of faith, which apprehends the forgiveness of sin. Here are the reasons why we say that the doctrine that contrition is a cause of the forgiveness of sins is a mingling of Law and Gospel:

1. Contrition is an effect solely of the Law. To regard contrition as a cause of the forgiveness of sins is equivalent to turning the Law into a message of grace and the Gospel into Law—a perversion which overthrows the entire Christian religion.

2. Contrition is not even a good work. For the contrition which precedes faith is nothing but suffering on the part of man. It consists of anguish, pain, torment, a feeling of being crushed; all of which God has wrought in man with the hammer of the Law. It is not an anguish which a person has produced in himself, for he would gladly be rid of it, but cannot, because God has come down on him with the Law, and he sees no way of escape from the ordeal. If a person sits down to meditate with a view to producing contrition in himself, he will never gain his object that way. He cannot produce contrition. Genuine repentance is produced by God only when the Law is preached in all sternness and man does not wilfully resist its influence.

Owing to their lack of experience many preachers are afraid they might lead people to despair. They do preach, as they should, that contrition must precede faith, but they fear that, unless they add some saving clause to that statement, one or the other member of their congregation may become despondent. For that reason they qualify their statement by saying that the pain one feels in contrition need not be very great, and that a person will be received by God if he only desires to be contrite. A comforting qualification of this kind really presents contrition as the cause of the forgiveness of sins, which is a false comfort. What the preacher ought to say is this: "Listen! When you have come to the point where you are hungering and thirsting for the grace of God, you have the contrition which you need. God does not require contrition as a means by which you are to atone for your sins, but only to the end that you may be roused from your security and ask, 'What must I do to be saved?'"

Accordingly, Luther says that, when he had for the first time grasped the meaning of the term *repentance,* no word seemed sweeter to him than that, because he perceived that its meaning was not that he must do penance for his sins, but simply that he must be alarmed on account of his sins and desire the mercy of God. The term *repentance* was to him the very Gospel, because he knew that the moment he had been brought by God to the point where he acknowledged himself to be a poor and lost sinner, he was a proper subject for the attention of Jesus and could go to Him with the assurance that He would receive him as he was, with all his sins and anguish and misery.

A person must not inquire whether his contrition is sufficient for admitting him to Jesus. His very question about his fitness shows that he may come to Jesus. If one has the desire to come to Jesus, he has true contrition even if he does not feel it. It is the same as when a person begins to believe.

The same mistake is made when a pastor is readily satisfied with a slight sign of contrition in his parishioners. In wicked men, who have lived a long time in sin and shame, the conscience may suddenly become aroused and charge them, for instance, with having perjured themselves. They are seized with palpitating fear because of the consequences. Or their conscience may reprove them with having soiled their hands with the blood of murder. However, these people are not alarmed because they regard themselves as poor sinners, but it is one particular sin that frightens them. Outside of that they imagine they are good at heart. There are many abandoned villains of this kind, who have already had their sentence of doom served on them. They may tell the pastor that they admit being at fault in this, that, or the other thing in which they slipped unavoidably, but they appeal to the fact that they are good at heart. If a pastor is satisfied with a partial contrition of this sort, he treats contrition as a merit.

Others say that contrition is necessary and that their own reason must tell them that God cannot forgive their sins which they treat so lightly. Then they proceed to describe to them what must be the quality of their contrition from texts like Ps. 38:6-8. Legalistic pastors will ask their client whether he can say all these things concerning himself, whether he has ever gone bowed down and mourning for a whole day, whether there has been a time when his loins were dried up, whether he can say that there was no sound part in his whole body, etc. Unless he can point to these criteria of what they regard as genuine contrition, they tell him not to imagine that he has been truly contrite.

This method is wrong. True, the text cited describes David's repentance. But where is there a text that prescribes the same *degree* of contrition for everyone? There is no such text; on the contrary, we find that when Peter's hearers on the first Pentecost were cut to the heart and they were moved to cry, "What shall we do?" the mercy of God was preached to them immediately. David's own case serves as an illustration. He had lived in impenitence for an entire year when Nathan came to hold his awful sin up to him. With a contrite heart David cried: "I have sinned against the Lord." That was all. The prophet Nathan noticed at once that David had been struck down and was crushed. Accordingly, he said to him: "The Lord also has put away your sin" (2 Sam. 12:13). The same thing we read about the jailer at Philippi. Only a few minutes before he had been so terribly agitated that he was about to take his own life. When he fell down before the apostles and cried, "Men, what must I do to be saved?" he was not told that he must produce contrition in himself, and that, a profound, a serious one; he was not reminded of the penitential acts of David, but he was promptly told: "Believe in the Lord Jesus Christ, and you will be saved, you and your household." The apostles saw plainly that the man was crushed and craved mercy, and they regarded that as sufficient. When a person has been made to hunger and thirst for mercy, contrition has done its full work in him.

If we may assume, in all reasonableness, that a person has been pried loose from his self-righteousness and wants to be saved by grace alone, we should for God's sake confidently preach the Gospel to him. It will not be too soon. A person cannot possibly come to Jesus too soon. The trouble is that people frequently do not really go to Jesus; they call themselves poor sinners, but are not; they want to bring before God some merit of their own. It is sheer hypocrisy when they say they are going to Jesus; for as a matter of fact they do not come to Him as poor beggars with all their sins. A person whom God has granted grace to see himself crushed and broken, without any comfort anywhere, and looking about him anxiously for consolation, such a one is truly contrite. He must not be warned against going to Jesus, but to him the Gospel must be preached. He must be told not only that he may, but that he should boldly come to Jesus and not imagine that he is coming too soon.

One of the principal reasons why many at this point mingle Law and Gospel is that they fail to distinguish the daily repentance of Christians from the repentance which precedes faith. Daily repentance is described in Ps. 51. David calls it a sacrifice which he brings before God and with which God is pleased. He does not speak of repentance which precedes faith, but of that which follows it. The great majority of sincere Christians who have the pure doctrine have a keener experience of repentance after faith than of repentance prior to faith. For, having good preachers, they have been led to Christ in no roundabout way. While they are with Christ, their former self-righteousness may make its appearance again, in spite of the fact that it has been shattered for them many a time. God must smite these poor Christians again and again to keep them humble. David's example may serve to illustrate this point. He had come to faith in a moment, but what misery did he have to pass through later! A prophet had spoken to him the word of the Lord, but to his dying day his heart was burdened with anguish, distress, and misery. God had ceased to prosper his undertakings; he met with one misfortune after the other, until God released him by death. But all that time David had contrition together with faith. That is, indeed, a sacrifice with which God is pleased.

Contrition of this kind is not a mere effect of the Law, produced by the Law alone, but it is at the same time an operation of the Gospel. By the Gospel the love of God enters a person's heart, and when contrition proceeds from love of God, it is indeed a truly sweet sorrow, acceptable to God. God is pleased with it; for we cannot accord Him greater honor than by casting ourselves in the dust before Him and confessing: "You are righteous, O Lord, but I am a poor sinner. Have mercy on me for the sake of Jesus Christ."

Thesis XIII

In the ninth place, the Word of God is not rightly divided when one makes an appeal to believe in a manner as if a person could make himself believe or at least help toward that end, instead of preaching faith into a person's heart by laying the Gospel promises before him.

This thesis does not score as an error the demand on the part of the pastor, be it ever so urgent, that his hearers believe the Gospel. That demand has been made by all the prophets, all the apostles, yes, by the Lord Jesus Christ Himself. When demanding faith, we do not lay down a demand of the Law, but issue the sweetest invitation, practically saying to our hearers: "Come, for all is now ready" (Luke 14:17). When I invite a half-starved person to sit down to a well-furnished board and to help himself to anything he likes, I do not expect him to tell me that he will take no orders from me. Even so the demand to believe is to be understood not as an order of the Law, but as an invitation of the Gospel.

The error against which this thesis is directed is that man can produce faith in himself. Such a demand would be an order of the Law and turn faith into a work of man. That would plainly be mingling Law and Gospel. A preacher must be able to preach a sermon on faith without ever using the term *faith*. It is not important that he din the word *faith* into the ears of his audience, but it is necessary for him to frame his address so as to arouse in every poor sinner the desire to lay the burden of his sins at the feet of the Lord Jesus Christ and say to Him: "You are mine, and I am Yours."

Here is where Luther reveals his true greatness. He rarely appeals to his hearers to believe, but he preaches concerning the work of Christ, salvation by grace, and the riches of God's mercy in Jesus Christ in such a manner that the hearers get the impression that all they have to do is to take what is being offered them and find a resting place in the lap of divine grace.

Suppose you were picturing to a horde of Indians the Lord Jesus, telling them that He is the Son of God who came down from heaven to redeem men from their sins by taking the wrath of God upon Himself, overcoming death, devil, and hell in their stead and opening heaven to all men, and that every man can now be saved by merely accepting what our Lord Jesus Christ has brought to us. Suppose that you were suddenly struck down by the deadly bullet of a hostile Indian lying in ambush. It is possible that, dying, you would leave behind you a small congregation of Indians though you may not even once have pronounced the word *faith* to them. For every one in that audience who did not wantonly and wilfully resist divine grace would have to reason that he, too, has been redeemed.

On the other hand, you may spend a lot of time telling men that they must believe if they wish to be saved, and your hearers may get the impression that something is required of them which they must do. They will begin to worry whether they will be able to do it, and when they have tried to do it, whether it is exactly the thing that is required of them. Thus you may have preached a great deal about faith without delivering a real sermon on faith. Anyone who has come to understand that it is up to him to accept what is offered him and actually accepts it, has faith. To be saved by faith means to acquiesce in God's plan of salvation by simply accepting it.

I do not mean to say that you must not preach about faith. Our time particularly lacks a proper understanding of this matter. The best preachers imagine they have accomplished a great deal when they have rammed into their hearers the axiom: "Faith alone saves." But by their preaching they have merely made their hearers sigh: "Oh, that I had faith! Faith must be something very difficult, for I have not obtained it." These unfortunate hearers will go home from church with a sad heart. The word *faith* is echoing in their ears but gives them no comfort.

To say that faith is required for salvation is not saying that man can produce faith himself. Scripture requires everything of man; every commandment is a demand crying: "Do this, and you will live." Scripture demands that we "purify our hearts" (James 4:8). We are told: "Awake, O sleeper, and arise from the dead, and Christ shall give you light" (Eph. 5:14). The mere issuing of such demands does not prove that man can comply with them. When a creditor demands payment, that does not prove that the debtor can pay. In ordinary daily life a creditor, knowing his debtor's insolvency, may demand payment of a debt merely because he has observed that the debtor is a shiftless person and, moreover, full of vanity and conceit. The creditor's object in making the demand is to get the debtor to quit his proud demeanor and to humble him. God deals with men the same way. By serving notice on me that I owe Him obedience to all His commandments, God leads me to realize that, even though I put forth my utmost endeavor, I cannot meet my obligations. Having humbled me, He then approaches me with His Gospel.

Thesis XIV

In the tenth place, the Word of God is not rightly divided when faith is required as a condition of justification and salvation, as if a person were righteous in the sight of God and saved, not only by faith, but also on account of his faith, for the sake of his faith, and in view of his faith.

What God's Word really means when it says that man is justified and saved by faith alone is nothing else than this: Man is *not saved by his own acts, but solely* by the doing and dying of his Lord and Savior Jesus Christ, the Redeemer of the whole world. Over against this teaching modern theologians assert that in the salvation of man two kinds of activity must be noted: in the first place, there is something that God must do. His part is the most difficult, for He must accomplish the task of redeeming men. But in the second place, something is required that man must do. For it will not do to admit persons to heaven, after they have been redeemed, without further parley. Man must do something really great — he has to believe. This teaching overthrows the Gospel completely.

Believing the Gospel would be, in truth, an immeasurably great and difficult task for us if God were not to accomplish it in us. But suppose it were not so exceedingly great and difficult; even if it were an easy condition that God had proposed to us for our salvation, our salvation would not be a gift; God would not have *given us His Son,* but merely offered Him to us with a certain stipulation. That has not been God's way. The apostle Paul says: "They are justified by His grace as a gift through the redemption which is in Christ Jesus" (Rom. 3:24). We are justified gratuitously without anything, even the least thing, being required of us. Accordingly, we poor sinners praise God for the place of refuge He has prepared for us, where we can flee even when we have to come to Him as utterly lost, insolvent beggars who have not the least ability to offer to God something they have achieved. All we can offer Him is our sins, nothing else. But for that very reason Jesus regards us as His proper clients. We honor Him as our faithful Savior by making His Gospel our refuge; but we deny Him if we come to Him offering Him something for what He gives us. In view of the statement of Peter: "There is salvation in no one else, for there is no other name under heaven given among men by which we must be saved" (Acts 4:12), you must regard it as an awful perversion of the Gospel to treat the command to believe as a condition of man's justification and salvation.

One is *not* saved *on account* of one's faith

Thesis XV

In the eleventh place, the Word of God is not rightly divided when the Gospel is turned into a preaching of repentance.

To understand these words correctly, you will have to bear in mind that the term *Gospel* has a usage similar to that of the term *repentance*. In the Holy Scriptures the term *repentance* is used in a wide and in a narrow sense. In the wide sense it signifies conversion viewed in its entirety, embracing knowledge of sin, contrition, and faith. This meaning occurs in Acts 2:38, where we read: "*Repent* and be baptized every one of you," etc. The apostle does not say: "Repent and believe." Accordingly, he refers to conversion in its entirety, inclusive of faith. Nor could he have said: "Be contrite and then be baptized." He must have conceived of contrition as joined with faith. What he means to say is this: If you acknowledge your sins and believe in the Gospel which I have just preached to you, then be baptized for the forgiveness of sins.

The term *repentance* is used in a narrow sense to signify the knowledge of sin and heartfelt sorrow and contrition. In Mark 1:15 we read: "Repent, and believe in the Gospel." In this statement John the Baptist evidently did not include faith in repentance; otherwise his statement would be tautological. In Acts 20:21 Paul relates that he had been "testifying both to Jews and to Greeks of repentance to God and of faith in our Lord Jesus Christ." Since faith is named *separately* in this text, the term *repentance* cannot embrace knowledge of sin, contrition, and faith. Likewise, the Lord says concerning the Jews that despite the preaching of John the Baptist they "did not afterward repent and believe him" (Matt. 21:32). By repentance he refers to the effects of the Law and means to say that, since they had not become alarmed over their sins, it had not been possible for them to believe. For there will not be faith in a heart that has not first been terrified.

There is a similar usage as regards the term *Gospel;* sometimes it is used in a wide, then again in a narrow meaning. The narrow meaning is its proper sense; in its wide meaning it is used merely by way of synecdoche, signifying anything that Jesus preached, including even His very poignant preaching of the Law, as, for instance, the Sermon on the Mount and His reproving of wicked men. Besides, the term *Gospel* is used in contradistinction to the Old Testament, which often signifies only the teaching of the Law.

Rom. 2:16: The apostle cannot refer to the Gospel in the narrow sense, for that has nothing to do with the Judgment, since Scripture declares: "He who believes in Him is not condemned" — "does not come into judgment" (John 3:18; 5:24). By *Gospel* in this text, Paul understands the doctrine which he had proclaimed and which was composed of both Law and Gospel.

The term *Gospel* is unquestionably used in the narrow sense in Rom. 1:16: It is called, first, a Gospel of Jesus Christ; next, a Gospel that saves *all that believe it.* No such demand is made upon us by the Law, which requires that we *keep* it. Accordingly, the apostle is here speaking of God's gift to the world and of faith, hence of the Gospel in the narrow sense, to the exclusion of the Law.

Eph. 6:15 speaks of *"the Gospel of peace."* Since the Law does not bring peace, but only unrest, the apostle in this text is speaking of the Gospel in the narrow sense, that is, of the glad tidings that Jesus Christ has come into the world to save sinners.

Our Lutheran Confessions follow the Bible in using the term *Gospel* now in the wide, now in the narrow sense. That explains the statement which occurs in them, viz.: "The Gospel preaches repentance." You will have to note this fact in order to understand our thesis correctly: a commingling of Law and Gospel takes place when the *Gospel of Christ,* that is, the Gospel in the narrow sense, is turned into a preaching of repentance.

It is not only extremely dangerous, but actually harmful to the souls of men for a minister to preach in such a manner as to lead men to believe that he regards the Gospel in its narrow and proper sense as a preaching of the Law and of the anger of God against sinners, calling them to repentance. Not to be cautious about the terms he uses is a great and serious fault even in a preacher whose personal faith may be correct.

I call attention to two additional objections to this thesis.

In the first place, it is objected that Scripture itself calls the Gospel a law and that, hence, the Gospel may be called a preaching unto repentance, because the Law serves the purpose of leading men to repentance. Rom. 3:27 is cited, where we read: "Where is boasting, then?

It is excluded. By what law? of works? Nay; but by *the law of faith.*"
According to the apostle's own terminology the objecters say that the
Gospel, too, is a law. This is drawing a faulty inference from the
apostle's words. The apostle in this passage employs the figure of
antanaclasis: he uses the same word which his opponent has used,
however in a different meaning, to refute the opponent.

Another objection is raised on the basis of Rom. 10:16: "They have
not all *obeyed* the Gospel." It is argued that, since it is really the Law
which enjoins obedience, the Gospel is not merely a message of joy,
but an improved law. However, it is an utter perversion of this text to
try to prove from it that the Gospel in the strict sense is a preaching
unto repentance. We are to obey the will of God not only as expressed
in the Law, but also His gracious will. But the latter is not a will of the
Law. By His gracious will, God offers and gives us all things. If we
accept what He gives, we are said to obey Him. It is an act of kindness
on God's part to call it obedience. And indeed, when we do obey Him
thus, we are also fulfilling the First Commandment, for faith is commanded in the Law, not in the Gospel. The Gospel is called "glad
tidings"; but glad tidings cannot be anything that imposes a task on me
which I am to perform. Only those tidings are good tidings which tell
me to put away all fear because God is gracious by advancing to meet
me.

Let us now take up the Bible passages which refer to the Gospel in
the strict sense, and learn by what marks we may know them.

1. Whenever the Gospel is contrasted with the Law, it is quite certain that the term *Gospel* does not refer to the Gospel in the wide, but
in the narrow sense.

Eph. 2:14-17: The preaching of the Law, which does not bring
peace, precedes and is followed by the Gospel, which brings peace.

2. Whenever the Gospel is presented as the peculiar teaching of
Christ or as the doctrine that proclaims Christ, it cannot refer to the
Law at the same time.

John 1:17: Jesus Christ did not first publish the Law, but He purged
the Law from the false interpretations of the Pharisees, because the
proper knowledge of the Law is necessary before a person is able to
accept the Gospel.

Luke 4:18-19: The Lord Jesus sets forth His mission to the world,
the real object of His preaching as Christ, the Savior of the world. He
concluded the foregoing statement by saying (v. 21): "Today this
scripture has been fulfilled in your hearing." He had not spoken to His
audience a word concerning the Law, but had only referred to the

doctrine that is offered to the poor, the sick, those of a bruised heart, and those in the bondage of sin and the devil.

3. Whenever poor sinners are named as the subject to whom the Gospel is addressed, the reference is to the Gospel in the strict sense. (Matt. 11:5; Luke 4:18)

4. Whenever forgiveness of sins, righteousness, and salvation by grace are named as effects of the Gospel, the reference is to the Gospel in the strict sense. (Rom. 1:16; Eph. 1:13)

5. When faith is named as the correlate of the Gospel, the reference is to the Gospel in the strict sense. (Mark 1:15; Mark 16:15-16)

Thesis XVI

In the twelfth place, the Word of God is not rightly divided when the preacher tries to make people believe that they are truly converted as soon as they have become rid of certain vices and engage in certain works of piety and virtuous practices.

The great importance of this thesis becomes apparent when you reflect that a worse commingling of Law and Gospel than that which is censured in this thesis is not possible. Woe to the minister who by his manner of preaching leads his hearers to imagine that they are good Christians if they have ceased robbing and stealing, and that by and by they will get rid of any weakness still remaining in them. They turn the Gospel into Law because they represent conversion as a work of man, while genuine conversion, which produces a living faith in a person, is effected only by the Gospel.

This grossest form of commingling Law and Gospel is the most grievous fault of rationalists. The essence of their religion is to teach men that they become different beings by putting away their vices and leading a virtuous life, while the Word of God teaches us that we must become different men first, and then we shall put away our particular sins and begin to exercise ourselves in good works. They love to cite the well-known saying: Genuine repentance is to quit doing what you have been doing. The saying can be used in a right sense and has been so used by our forefathers. They meant to say: "You people who boast of having the right faith while you lead wicked lives, hush your prating about faith; quitting what you have been doing, that is genuine repentance." The meaning which rationalists connect with the saying is this: "Do not worry; what God requires of a true Christian is that he quit doing what he has been doing. That is genuine repentance." That is the abominable teaching of moralists. The Christian religion gives us the correct teaching in one word: μετανοεῖτε, which means: "Change your mind." With this word the Lord confronts the sinner, telling him that, first of all, a change of his innermost self must take place. What He requires is a new mind, a new heart, a new spirit; not quitting vice and

CHICKEN OR EGG?
① PUT AWAY VICES → CHRISTIAN (NEW PEOPLE)
✓ ② NEW PEOPLE → PUT AWAY VICES
(INNER CHANGE)   (OUTER CHANGE)

doing good works. By making this the primary requisite for being a Christian, He puts the ax to the root of the evil tree.

John 3:3: The Lord meant to say: "All that you undertake to do while still in your carnal nature is sin; you must become spiritual before genuine spiritual fruits will begin to show themselves in your life."

Matt. 12:33: Unless a person is completely changed, unless he has become a new creature, has been born anew, with a new mind, all his doings will be corrupt fruit; for by nature every man is a corrupt tree.

Matt. 15:13: Only those works which God has wrought are good. Any work which a person has produced by the power of his reason and natural will is a plant that will have to be rooted up. God will not recognize it, but demand that it be removed out of His sight as a sin and an abomination, because it has sprung from a corrupt heart, a heart that cares nothing for God.

1 Cor. 13:3: What is all-important are not the works themselves, but the love from which they proceed. I may be so abjectly poor that I am not able to do anything, and yet in God's estimate I may abound in good works if, while I am suffering poverty according to the will of God, love awakens in me the desire to do good to all men.

Even believing pastors may, without being aware of it, slip into a horrible commingling of Law and Gospel, not so much in their sermons as in their private ministrations and in the exercise of church discipline. Many pastors and congregations make mistakes in applying church discipline. They may be dealing with a drunkard who readily professes sorrow over his sins, as these people usually do. An inexperienced minister is easily deceived by such a profession. The drunkard may be suspended from church membership and placed under surveillance for three months. Presently some brother brings the good news that the drunkard has kept himself sober all that time, and the minister decides that the drunkard is now converted, while in reality he is still quite a godless person. Beware of being deceived thus! The same may happen when a habitually profane person who has been admonished by the congregation quits cursing for a while. Or take the case of a person who is negligent in church attendance, who therefore certainly is not a Christian. After he has been brought before the congregation, he may come to church for several successive Sundays. But does this outward act alone make him a Christian? By no means; any godless person is able to do what such a one is doing. The aforementioned persons must be made to realize that no Christian acts like them; if he does, he cannot possibly be in a state of grace. But it requires labor on the part of the minister till these persons are reborn by the Word of God. If he is unwilling to perform this labor, he neglects the souls of such persons. — Or take the case of tardy communicants who will come to the Sacrament once again after the minister has reproved them. If he is satisfied with that, he is guilty of commingling Law and Gospel. Or take the sin of avarice. A congregation may be so stingy as to refuse to take up a collection; it may fail to pay the pastor his salary. In that case the pastor must not resolve to preach his people a sharp sermon in order to open their purses. Opening purses by means of the Law is no achievement at all. He must preach in a manner that will rouse them out of their spiritual sleep and death. If he does not do that, he falls under the censure of our sixteenth thesis.

Luther insists that in a regenerate person everything that he does is God's work. Even when he treats himself to a hearty meal, eats or sleeps, he is doing a good work, not only when he engages in hard labor. A servant of the Law may slave and slave, but all his activities are a martyrdom that is preparing him for perdition. A Christian has the right mind in all that he does; therefore all his actions are God-pleasing. From a pure fountain nothing but good, sweet water can flow.

Thesis XVII

In the thirteenth place, the Word of God is not rightly divided when a description is given of faith, both as regards its strength and the consciousness and productiveness of it, that does not fit all believers at all times.

Young ministers who are still without great experience frequently make this mistake. They desire to make an impression on their people and rouse them out of their natural security. They imagine that, in order to prevent hypocrites from regarding themselves as Christians, they cannot raise the demands which they make upon those who are Christians too high. However, here is a point where the minister must be careful not to go beyond the Word of God, or by reason of his zeal he will inflict awful harm on the souls of his hearers. Christians are in many respects quite different from the descriptions, bona fide descriptions at that, which are given of them in sermons. The minister wants to rouse his people and warn them against self-deception. However, that cannot be his *ultimate aim.* His ultimate aim must be to lead his hearers to the assurance that they have forgiveness of sins with God, the hope of the future blessed life, and confidence to meet death cheerfully. Anyone who does not make these things his ultimate aim is not an evangelical minister. For this reason he must be careful, for God's sake, not to say: "Anyone who does this or that is not a Christian," unless he is quite sure of his ground. Frequently a Christian may act in a very unchristian manner. ✚✚✚

Rom. 7:18: The apostle describes a Christian as a double being. The true Christian always desires what is good, but frequently he does not accomplish it. Now, then, if a preacher describes a Christian as if he does not really will what is good unless he accomplishes all of it, the description is unbiblical. To will what is good is the main trait of a Christian. Frequently he does not progress beyond the good will to do something. Before he is aware of it, he has gone astray; the sin within him has come forth, and he is ashamed of himself. But for that reason he has not by any means fallen from grace.

Rom. 7:14: The Christian feels like a slave, with this difference, however, that he does *not* obey his master *gladly* as a *Christian* slave must obey. He renders obedience with the utmost reluctance. Accordingly, the apostle cries in v. 24: "Wretched man that I am! Who will deliver me from this body of death?" Now, when a real Christian is shown what a miserable sinner he is, he clings to Christ all the more firmly and spurns the whispering of the devil, who tells him that he is fallen from grace and has lost God.

Phil. 3:12: In this life we follow after, but we do not apprehend. It may seem to a Christian that there were times when he was holier and could overcome sin better. That may actually have been the case, and his present condition may be due to his spiritual retrogression. But the correct explanation of his present state may also be that he sees much more plainly now what a frail being he is.

Gal. 5:17: A minister has no right to denounce a person as an unchristian because he is not doing all that he should, as long as the person maintains that he does not will his imperfections. If he commits sin from weakness or in rashness, he can still be a Christian.

James 3, 2: A Christian sins not only in thoughts, desires, gestures, and words, but also in his actions, which makes it evident to all the world that he is still a poor, weak man.

Heb. 12:1: A Christian is always putting away sin, which besets him continually. He cannot get it out of his heart, and it makes him so very sluggish. His conduct would be quite different, he would walk cheerfully with his God like a hero, if he did not have to lug his carnal mind with him.   +++

Our Savior taught all Christians to offer up this daily petition in the Lord's Prayer: "Forgive us our trespasses." Every day puts a new burden of guilt on our heart and conscience. To represent a Christian as he is not, namely perfect, or to enumerate marks of a true Christian which are not found in all Christians, means to misrepresent a Christian and will do infinite harm. For from such characterizations Christians with a very live conscience will draw the conclusion that they are no Christians. Therefore the minister must furnish Christians the proper remedy when they sin, promptly to rise from their fall, provided their sin is not intentional; for an intentional sin would indeed drive the Holy Spirit from them. But a Christian learns by experience to sense danger; and when he has sinned, he feels himself urged promptly to seek his Father in heaven, confess his sin, and ask to be forgiven for Jesus' sake. He also feels inwardly assured that he has been forgiven.

Frequently the Christian is pictured as patient as Job. The preacher

FALSE PICTURES OF TRANS

80

will say: "You may take everything away from a Christian, and he will cheerfully say: 'The Lord gave, and the Lord has taken away; blessed be the name of the Lord'" (Job 1:21), and the preacher may think that his remarks have been quite Biblical. Job did indeed say those words, but not all Christians say them. It is not consistent with truth to set up such a claim in a sermon. Many a Christian grows impatient in trouble. His impatience may become violent even over trifling matters. When he spiritually comes to again, as it were, he is ashamed of himself.

It cannot be said to be a criterion of a Christian that he never commits a gross sin. That does happen occasionally; but whenever this is the case, the Christian surrenders unconditionally to the Word of God, even though he may not do so immediately. He may at first be so blinded by the devil that he believes he is right. Finally, however, God's Word convinces him that he was wrong, and then he humbly asks forgiveness, while a hypocrite persists as long as he can in the claim that he has done right.

Many preachers picture the Christian as a person who does not fear death. That is a serious misrepresentation, because the great majority of Christians are afraid to die. If a Christian does not fear death and declares that he is ready to die at any time, God has bestowed a special grace upon him. Some have expressed this sentiment before their physician told them that they would not live another night, but after that they were seized with a terrible fear.

Do not, for God's sake, draw a false picture of a Christian; but whenever you have drawn the picture of a Christian, see whether you can recognize yourself in that picture.

Even pride in a very pronounced form can crop out in a Christian, and that is one of the worst vices, because it is a transgression of the First Commandment. By nature we are all proud; only one is more strongly inclined to that sin than another. Persons of a choleric temperament, possessing what is called a strong will and great energy, as a rule have a great deal of self-confidence and expect others to show them reverential regard—a result of abominable pride. This sin sometimes crops out even in true Christians. Observe the disciples of the Lord quarreling with one another about who was the greatest among them. If this incident had not been recorded in the Bible, we could hardly believe that the apostles quarreled like children about their superiority and that the mother of Zebedee's sons requested that one of them be placed at the right and the other at the left hand of the Lord. From the account in Luke we gather that the disciples were ill at ease during this quarrel because they knew that their conduct was shameful, and when the Lord rebuked them, they felt so deeply ashamed that they would have liked to hide themselves.

Again, it is wholly incorrect and false to picture the Christian as being always fervent in prayer and as if praying were his most cherished occupation. It is not so; it takes much struggling on the part of the Christian to make him fit for prayer, fervent in it, and confident that he will really obtain from God what he is praying for. Though there are times when the Christians' flesh and blood are forced into the background and they feel as if they were dissolving in happiness, as if they were in heaven and conversing with God, they nevertheless retain their natural flesh and blood.

Christians are even tempted with the desire to grow rich. If they were not warned and admonished, they would be dragged into perdition as if caught in a snare, and would be lost forever.

In judging any person, it is of decisive importance to know whether he loves the Word of God and his Savior or whether he is hardened and leads a shameful life. There are people who want to make a show of great sanctity by avoiding conversation, raising their eyes piously to heaven, citing Scripture continually, and reading their Bible in leisure hours in order to impress people with their exemplary Christianity. We must not think that only those are true Christians who make a display of godliness. I do not assert that every one of these people is an unchristian, but I am sure that such as are wholly given to the aforementioned practices are miserable hypocrites. Read the gospels and note how the disciples conversed with the Lord and how they acted in His presence. They expressed their minds plainly, even John, the beloved disciple. Christ did not for that reason denounce them as unconverted, but treated them as converted people who, however, still carried a pretty vigorous portion of the Old Adam with them.

You may, in your sermons, refer to actions of *strong* or exceptionally *faithful* Christians. It will not harm your hearers to think that they have not yet attained to such a degree of faithfulness; it will rather prove an incentive to them to make better progress in their Christianity.

When new members are to be received into the congregation and you have to talk to them, you must not regard them as godless, unconverted people if they do not immediately engage in a religious conversation with you. There are people who cling to their Savior, but are unable to talk much about their faith, although on other topics they may be ready talkers. Others, again, may not have much experience and for that reason may not be able to say much.

Thesis XVIII

In the fourteenth place, the Word of God is not rightly divided when the universal corruption of mankind is described in such a manner as to create the impression that even true believers are still under the spell of ruling sins and are sinning purposely.

I am speaking of the claim that the universal corruption of mankind embraces living in dominant and willful sins on the part of believers. No one who is conversant with the pure doctrine will make the unqualified assertion that a Christian can be a fornicator and an adulterer. Such a thought would not enter the mind of a true teacher of the Word of God. But a preacher trying to give a very drastic description of the universal corruption of mankind is easily tempted to deviate from the pure doctrine. What damage can be done when people are made to hear that we human beings are living in every abomination, shame, and vice, without the qualifying statement: "as we are by nature" or: "as long as a person is still in the state of natural depravity and is unregenerate." With these qualifiers, of course, you cannot overdraw the horrible qualities of man's natural condition. However, when addressing a Christian congregation, you will have to be very careful not to speak as if also all Christians were living in shame and vice. It was a harmful and dangerous attempt on the part of the Pietists to divide mankind into so many classes that nobody was able to tell in which class he belonged. But this must not keep us from pointing out in our sermons the two great classes into which mankind is really divided, viz., believers and unbelievers, godly and ungodly, converted and unconverted, regenerate and unregenerate persons. This classification is current throughout the Scriptures. See Mark 16:16; Matt. 5:45; 9:13; 13:38. Your hearers must learn that they are either spiritually dead or spiritually alive, either converted or unconverted, either under the wrath of God or in a state of grace, either Christians or unchristians, either asleep in sin or quickened to a new life in God, subjects in either the devil's or God's kingdom.

There are but two goals at the end of this life — heaven and hell.

There will be only two sentences pronounced on men, either unto damnation or unto eternal life. Accordingly, there are only two classes of men in the present life; those of the one class are headed direct for hell, those of the other, straight for heaven (Matt. 7:13-14). To confound these two classes of men is an abominable mingling of Law and Gospel. The Law produces reprobate sinners, the Gospel free and blessed men.

Rom. 6:14: Sin will not be able to dominate Christians. It is absolutely impossible that a person who is in a state of grace should be ruled by sin.

1 Cor. 6:7-11: No one, then, who falls into the aforementioned sins and fails to repent of them shall inherit the kingdom of God. The Christian's repentance consists in this, that he desires to commit these sins no more. Whoever commits these sins intentionally has, by that token, a proof that he is not a Christian but a reprobate who is moved, not by the Spirit of God but by the hellish spirit.

2 Peter 2:20-22: The apostle Peter is here speaking of persons who had been children of God, had had a living knowledge of the Lord Jesus, and had been in a state of divine grace. How, then, can anyone be so bold as to assert that a person who had been truly converted stays converted even when, like Peter and David, he falls into some particular sin?

Rom. 8:13-14: Those who are not led by the Spirit of God, but by their flesh, are not the children of God, but servants of Satan.

Thesis XIX

In the fifteenth place, the Word of God is not rightly divided when the preacher speaks of certain sins as if they are not of a damnable, but of a venial nature.

We have already seen that a distinction must be made between mortal and venial sins. A person failing to make this distinction does not rightly divide Law and Gospel. But the distinction between these two kinds of sin must be made with great care. It must be clearly shown that the distinction is made for the purpose of proving that certain sins expel the Holy Ghost from the believer. When the Holy Spirit is driven out, faith, too, is ejected; for no one can come to faith nor retain it without the Holy Ghost. Sins which expel the Holy Ghost and bring on spiritual death are called *mortal sins.* Anyone who has been a Christian will readily perceive when the Holy Spirit has departed from him by his inability to offer up childlike prayers to God and to resist sin stoutly and bravely as he used to do. He will feel as if he had become chained to sin, like a slave. It is a good thing if he has at least this knowledge of his condition, for thus he may be brought back to God. But while this condition endures, he is not in communion with God.

Venial sins are termed such as a Christian commits without forfeiting the indwelling of the Holy Spirit. They are sins of weakness or rashness; frequently they are called the daily sins of Christians.

We must be scrupulously careful not to create the notion that venial sins are sins about which a person need not be greatly concerned and for which he does not have to ask forgiveness. It happens only too often that preachers create the impression that to Christians venial sins are matters over which they need not worry. Since all are sinners and no one ever gets rid of sin entirely, there is no reason why one should feel disturbed because of these sins. Such talk, however, is really awful and ungoldly.

Matt. 5:18-19: The connection in which the Lord uttered these words is worthy of note. In the words preceding them He states that

85

He has come to fulfill the Law. Now, inasmuch as the Lord had to fulfill every law and every commandment in our stead, it is shocking in any man, poor, sinful worm that he is, to want to dispense with a single law of God and to treat it as a matter of no importance. Those who entertain notions of this kind are no Christians. If any man has manufactured for himself some secret comfort from his notion, he has miserably belied and cheated himself. Also in this matter a true Christian manifests himself as a person who fears to commit a single sin.

The Lord also speaks of a person "who shall *teach* men so." It is bad enough when a person for his own part disregards some law and leads a careless life; but it is much worse when he preaches his lax views and leads men to perdition by his preaching. He will have to render an account to God of his preaching, and on that day he may not excuse himself by claiming that it was only trifling matters which he had represented as so unimportant that no one need grieve over them. A Christian grieves even over trifles, but unchristians imagine that they can "escape by iniquities," Ps. 56, 7.

Matt. 12:36: By a concrete example we are shown how abominable it is to speak of sins which are in themselves venial and are automatically remitted by God, because He does not regard them as a great evil. Those who speak thus represent God, the Holy and Righteous, as a feeble, old man like Eli, who saw his sons sin and merely said, "No, my sons!" (1 Sam. 2:24) thinking that therewith he had done his full duty. True, God is Love, but He is also Holiness and Righteousness. To the person who rises up against Him God becomes a terrible fire, and His fiery wrath pursues the sinner into the lowest hell. Any evil word for which a sinner is tried on Judgment Day is sufficient for his condemnation. Now, is there a Christian who can say at the end of a day on which he has spoken much that he has not uttered a single idle word? Few Christians will be able to say that. Even for an idle word Christians must ask God's pardon with a contrite heart and promise to guard their lips better in the future. If God were not to forgive their idle words, these alone would damn them. There is no sin venial in itself; but there are such sins as will not hinder a person from still believing in Jesus Christ with all his heart.

James 2:10: If a person had kept nine hundred and ninety-nine out of a thousand commandments, he would be guilty of the whole Law. That applies to every one of the so-called venial sins. Unless a Christian clearly understands this fact, he ceases to be a Christian. What makes a person a Christian is this believing knowledge, that he is, in the first place, a miserable, accursed sinner, who would be lost forever if Christ had not died for him; and that, in the second place, Jesus Christ, true God, begotten of the Father in eternity, and also true man, born of the Virgin Mary, has redeemed him, a lost and condemned creature, purchased and won him from all sins, from death, and from the power of the devil. A Christian must regard himself as a lost and condemned sinner, or all his talk about faith is vain and worthless.

Gal. 3:10: The curse will descend on everyone that does not continue to do *all* things that are written in the Book of the Law. Hence there can be no sin that is venial by its nature. Sins are venial only for Christ's sake.

1 John 1:7: The apostle says "from all sin," not "from all mortal sins, all grievous sins, all gross sins." Hence, the blood of Jesus Christ, the Son of God, must have been required also for canceling the so-called venial sins. That being so, venial sins *in themselves* must also be mortal sins. Sin is something awful, because it is lawlessness. It is rebellion against the holy, omnipotent God, our supreme, heavenly Lawgiver.

Matt. 5:21-22: Is there a Christian who need not blame himself for having been angry at his brother, even though it was not for a long time? It was done in weakness; nevertheless he has committed a sin of which he has to be ashamed. When Christ says: "He is in danger of the Judgment," He treats anger and murder alike. The term "raca" signifies that anger in the heart breaks forth in angry words and gestures. It reaches its worst stage when the angry person cries, "Thou fool!" The Law promptly consigns such an angry person to hellfire.

All these texts prove that the so-called venial sins are not venial in themselves, in their nature, but damnable, mortal sins. Only of the believer it is written: "There is therefore now no condemnation for those who are in Christ Jesus" (Rom. 8:1); but a believer is the very person who regards sin as a very serious matter.

Evangelical preaching means that sin must be magnified. The minister must pronounce a severe judgment on sin, for He is to proclaim the judgment of God. Also venial sins you must not regard lightly. You must remember that you sin so much every day that God would have to cast you into hell, but that He will not do it because you believe in Christ. Always remind yourselves that, if God were to deal with you according to His justice, you would belong in hell. You are to be in such fear and behave in such a way as if you were full of deadly trespasses.

Finally, Christian experience also proves that in its nature no sin is venial. Any true Christian will tell you this to be his experience, that, as soon as he had sinned, he felt an unrest, which continued until he had asked God for forgiveness. In every true Christian the conscience promptly rings an alarm.

Thesis XX

In the sixteenth place, the Word of God is not rightly divided when a person's salvation is made to depend on his association with the visible orthodox church and when salvation is denied to every person who errs in any article of faith.

It seems strange that men should have hit upon the doctrine that the visible Lutheran Church is the church outside of which there is no salvation. The mother of the awful error which we are studying is the doctrine that the church is a visible institution which Christ has established on earth, differing in no way from a religious state. Its governing offices are superintendents, bishops, church councils, pastors, deacons, synods, and the like. That *this view is erroneous,* everyone who is at least somewhat conversant with God's Word knows. Does not the Savior say: "On this rock I will build My church, and the powers of death shall not prevail against it" (Matt. 16:18)? This rock is Christ. No one is a member of the church except he who is built upon Christ. Being built upon Christ does not mean connecting oneself mechanically with the church, but putting one's confidence in Christ and hoping to obtain righteousness and salvation from Him alone. Whoever fails to do this is not built on this rock, hence is not a member of the church of Jesus Christ.

Eph. 2:19-22: No one is built upon the foundation of the apostles and prophets who does not believingly cling to their word. Hence, no one is a member of the church who is without a living faith.

The Savior calls Himself a bridegroom. Let no one who is not betrothed to Christ with the innermost affection of his heart claim to be a true Christian and a member of the church. As regards his relation to Christ, he is an alien; the church, however, is the bride of Christ.

Again, Christ is called the Head of the church. Hence only he can be a member of the church into whom there flows from Christ, the Head, light, life, strength, and grace. Whoever is not in this spiritual connection with Christ has not Christ for his Head. Whoever is his own ruler and is not governed by Christ does not belong to the church.

In another place the apostle calls the church the body of Christ.

This has prompted many even of the most faithful Lutherans to say that, since a body is visible, the church, too, must be visible. But that is an abominable piece of exegesis. The point of comparison in the aforementioned phrase is not the visibility of the church, but that, instead of being composed of many dead instruments, it is a vital organism of members in whom *one* faith and one energy of faith is pulsating. This proves beyond contradiction that the church is not visible, but invisible. Only he is a member of the church who experiences the constant outflowing of energy from Christ, the Head of the church.

Again, Christ calls the church His flock. Hence no one is a member of the church who does not belong to the flock of Christ, is not one of His sheep, pastured by Him and obeying His voice.

The objection is raised that Christ compares the church to a field in which wheat and tares are growing. But the objection is owing to a wrong interpretation of the parable. Christ has given us the key that unlocks its meaning. He does not say: "The field is My kingdom." In that case the church would be a society composed of good and evil members. But He says: "The field is the world" (Matt. 13:38). The Apology of the Augsburg Confession emphasizes this fact. The Savior likens His church to a field in which tares grow together with the wheat; to a net in which good and bad fishes are caught; to a marriage feast to which foolish virgins come with others, and to which, according to another parable, one gained entrance who is not dressed in the proper wedding garment. By means of all these parables Christ does not mean to describe the essence of the church, but the outward form in which it appears in this world and its lot among the men of this world: although it is composed only of good sheep, only of regenerate persons, still it never presents itself in the form of a congregation that is made up of none but true Christians. In its visible form the church can never purge itself of hypocrites and ungodly persons, who find their way into it. Not until its consummation in the life eternal will the church appear triumphant, entirely purified and without blemish, separated from those who were not honestly and sincerely joined to it but only sought their own secular interest in an outward union with the church. While hypocrites and sham Christians profess Christ with their lips, their heart is far from Him. They are serving their carnal lusts and not the Lord alone. In Luke 14:26 the Lord says: "If anyone comes to Me and does not hate his own father and mother and wife and children and brothers and sisters, yes, and even his own life, he cannot be My disciple." In this passage Christ passes judgment on all who do not want to renounce what they have. But not until all are gathered before the judgment seat of Christ will these people become known as hypocrites. *We may see people going to church, but we cannot see whether they belong to the church.* It is impossible to declare regarding individuals that they are true members of the church. No man, but only God, knows whether they are. To the eyes of God alone the church is visible; to the eyes of men it is invisible.

The error we are now discussing is the primary falsehood of our time. For those who are addicted to this error pretend to be good Lutherans, opposed to the papists, and yet they have only changed weapons with the papists. Formerly the papists defended the false doctrine now under review; now Lutherans dare to set up the claim against them that the Lutherans are the church outside of which there is no salvation. The only inferences that can be drawn from this state of affairs would be, either that the pope's church is the true church or that the true church had perished before Luther came. But Scripture says that the true church cannot perish; it shall continue until the end of time. Now, until the sixteenth century there was no church denominated "Lutheran." In fact, no church since the days of the apostles has had the pure doctrine as our fathers had it. Hence, either Scripture has lied or the Roman Church was the true church and Luther's reformation was rebellion. That is the vexing dilemma in which all those are placed who wish to maintain the false doctrine concerning the church sketched above.

Its worst feature, however, is undeniably this: Making a person's salvation depend on this membership in, and communion with, the visible orthodox church means to overthrow the doctrine of justification by faith. True faith has been obtained by people before they join the Lutheran Church. It is a fatal mistake to think that Luther before becoming a Lutheran did not have the true faith. Though we esteem our church highly, may this abominable fanatical notion be far from us, that our Lutheran Church is the alone-saving church! The true church extends throughout the world and is found in all sects; for it is not an external organism with peculiar arrangements to which a person must adapt himself in order to become a member of the church. Anyone who believes in Jesus Christ and is a member of His spiritual body is a member of the church. This church, moreover, is never divided; although its members are separated from one another by space and time, the church is ever one.

A false inference is drawn from the fact that Scripture speaks of external ecclesiastical communities, such as those at Rome, Corinth,

Philippi, Thessalonica, in Galatia, and those in Asia Minor to whom the Lord issued letters through St. John. All these visible communities are called churches. Hence it is claimed that the church is visible. – Now, Luther, in order to keep people from imagining that the pope is the church, has translated ἐκκλησία by "congregation," which is a correct rendering. The inference drawn from the use of this term when applied to local churches is wrong, because the Scriptures, as a rule, employ this term when referring to no local congregation, but to the church in the absolute sense, and that is an invisible community. The term is applied to local organizations because the invisible church is contained in them. In a similar manner we speak of a stack of wheat, although it is not all wheat, but a good deal of hay and straw is in the pile. Or we speak of a glass of wine, although water has been mixed with it. In such instances the object is denominated from its principal content. Thus visible communities are called "churches" because the invisible church is in them, because they contain a heavenly seed. False Christians and hypocrites are given the name of "members of the congregation," when in reality they are not members. Since they confess the name of Jesus, we apply to them this title charitably, assuming that they believe what they confess.

Now, the Lutheran Church too, as a visible community, is called a "church" in a synecdochical sense. It is, therefore, an awful mistake to claim that men can be saved only in the Lutheran Church. No one must be induced to join the Lutheran Church because he thinks that only in that way he can get into the church of God. We have this promise in Is. 55:11: "My Word . . . shall not return to Me empty." Wherever the Word of God is proclaimed and confessed or even recited during the service, the Lord is gathering a people for Himself. The Roman Church, for instance, still confesses that Christ is the Son of God and that He died on the cross to redeem the world. That is truth sufficient to bring a man to the knowledge of salvation. Whoever denies this fact is forced to deny also that there are Christians in some Lutheran communities in which errors have cropped out. There are always some children of God in these communities because they have the Word of God, which is always bearing fruit in converting some souls to God.

The false doctrine concerning the church which we are studying involves a fatal confounding of Law and Gospel. While the Gospel requires faith in Jesus Christ, the Law makes all sorts of demands upon men. Setting up a demand of some kind as necessary to salvation in addition to faith, the acceptance of the Gospel promises, means to commingle Law and Gospel. I belong to the Lutheran Church for the sole reason that I want to side with the truth. I quit the church to which I belong when I find that it harbors errors with which I do not wish to be contaminated. I do not wish to become a partaker of other men's sins, and by quitting a heretical community I confess the pure and unadulterated truth. For Christ says: "Everyone who acknowledges Me before men, I also will acknowledge before My Father who is in heaven; but whoever denies Me before men, I also will deny before My Father who is in heaven" (Matt. 10:32-33). Again, Paul writes distinctly to Timothy: "Do not be ashamed then of testifying to our Lord, nor of me His prisoner." (2 Tim. 1:8)

From the fact that men may be saved in all the sects and that in all sectarian churches there are children of God, it by no means follows that one can remain in communion with a sect. Many people cannot comprehend this; they imagine it is an utterly unionistic principle to hold that a person can be saved in any of the sects. But it is true, and the reason is that we are saved by faith, which some members of sectarian churches may have. However, if I perceive the error of my heretical community and do not forsake it, I shall be lost because, though seeing the error, I would not abandon it.

The Lutheran Church is indeed the true visible church; however, only in this sense, that it has the pure, unadulterated truth. As soon as you add the qualification "alone-saving" to the Lutheran Church, you detract from the doctrine of justification by grace through faith in Jesus Christ and confound Law and Gospel.

Thesis XXI

In the seventeenth place, the Word of God is not rightly divided when men are taught that the sacraments produce salutary effects ex opere operato, *that is, by the mere outward performance of a sacramental act.*

The grave error which is scored by this thesis is held by the papists, who teach men that they will derive some benefit by merely submitting to the act of being baptized, despite the fact that they are still unbelievers, provided they are not actually living in mortal sins. That mere act is said to bring them God's favor or make God gracious to them. They teach the same regarding the Mass and the Lord's Supper, viz., that grace is obtained by the mere act of attending these rites. This teaching contradicts the Word of God, in particular, the Gospel, which teaches that a person is justified before God and saved by grace alone, and that he cannot perform any good work until he has been thus justified.

Rom. 3:28: If I am justified, if I obtain grace by my act of submitting to baptizing or by my act of going to Communion, I am justified by works, and at that altogether paltry works, scarcely worth mentioning. For that is what Baptism and Holy Communion are when viewed as works that we perform. It is a horrible doctrine, wholly contradicting the Bible, that divine grace is obtained if a person at least makes external use of the sacraments. The truth is that Baptism and Holy Communion place any person under condemnation who does not approach them with faith in his heart. They are means of grace only for the reason that a divine promise has been attached to an external symbol. Having water poured on me is of no benefit to me. Nor am I benefited by actually receiving the body and blood of the Lord in the Holy Supper. I am rather harmed by going to Communion without faith, because I become guilty of the body and blood of the Lord. It is of paramount importance that I believe, that I regard, not the water in Baptism, but the promise which Christ has attached to the water. It is this promise that requires the water; for only to it has the promise been attached.

The same applies to the Holy Supper: it is impious to imagine that the act of approaching the Lord's Table, doing something that the Lord wants done, is one more merit that He will have to credit to our account. The Lord says: "Take, eat; this is My body, *which is given for you.*" "Drink of it, all of you; this cup is the new testament in My blood, *which is shed for you for the remission of sins.*" These words open up a heaven full of divine grace to the communicant, and to these words he must direct his faith. The mere act of eating the bread with the body of Christ and of drinking the wine with the blood of Christ produces no good effect in us. Grace does not operate in a chemical or in a mechanical manner, but only by the Word, by virtue of God's saying continually: "Your sins are forgiven you." To this word I must cling by faith. If I do that, I can confidently meet God on the Last Day; and if He were preparing to condemn me, I could say to Him: "You cannot condemn me without making Yourself a liar. You have invited me to place my entire confidence in Your promise. I have done that, and therefore I cannot be condemned, and I know You will not do it." If God were to try the faith of His Christians even on the Last Day, all His saints would cry: "It is impossible that we should be consigned to perdition. Here is Christ, our Surety and Mediator. You will have to acknowledge, O God, the ransom which Your Son has given as payment in full for our sin and guilt."

Rom. 14:23: How, then, can a person who uses the sacraments without faith become acceptable to God by that act or obtain God's grace by it, since he is committing a sin by doing something that does not proceed from faith?

In this connection the statement, too, deserves to be pondered that is recorded concerning the working of God's Word on the inner powers of man, Heb. 4, 12.

False teachers admit that preaching, unless it is received by faith, does not benefit the hearers but rather increases their responsibility. However, they claim, the situation is different as regards the sacraments, since these have, they say, this great advantage over the preached Word, that God operates with His grace through them whenever men merely use them. That is an impious doctrine, because the sacraments are nothing else than the Word of God attached to a symbol. Augustine beautifully calls them the visible Word. The Word of God does not benefit a person who does not believe. Even so an unbeliever is not benefited by going through the action of being baptized. When we urge men to believe in their Baptism, the meaning is that they are to believe their heavenly Father, who has attached such a glorious promise to Baptism. The idea that God is highly pleased when a person offers his head to have water sprinkled on it is an abominable misuse of the visible Word. As the Word does not benefit a person who does not believe, even so the sacraments help only those who embrace them by faith.

The Gospel merely says: "Believe, and you will be saved," while the Law issues the order: "Do this, and you will live." Now, if the mere act of being baptized and partaking of Holy Communion brings grace to a person, the Gospel manifestly has been turned into a law, because salvation then rests on a person's works. Moreover, the Law has been turned into a gospel, because salvation is promised a person as a reward for his works.

One would indeed think it to be utterly impossible for a Christian minister to teach that the sacraments produce salutary effects *ex opere operato;* still, that is what happens again and again. This awful error is taught by the very men who wish to pass for genuinely strict Lutherans, every time they discuss the sacraments. When they have finished unfolding their doctrine of Baptism, every hearer has received the unmistakable impression that, in order to get to heaven, it is merely necessary to submit to the act of being baptized. When they have finished their presentation of the doctrine of the Lord's Supper, the people are convinced that, to obtain the forgiveness of sins, all that a person has to do is to take Communion, because God has attached His grace to this external action.

If the Word that is preached will not benefit a person unless he believes it, neither will being baptized and taking Communion benefit anyone without faith. Telling a person that he will be saved by faith means nothing else than that he will be saved by grace. Most people express the matter thus: "If you wish to be saved, you must perform this task and that, but you must not omit to *believe.* That is what God requires of you." Over against this notion remember Rom. 4:16: "Therefore it [righteousness] is *of faith* that it might be *by grace.*" Any teaching that is set up contrary to the doctrine that man is not saved by his works, his running, or any effort of his own, but by grace alone, is an error that subverts the foundation of the Christian doctrine. "You must believe" means: "You must accept what is offered you." Our Father in heaven offers men forgiveness of sins, righteousness, life, and salvation. But of what benefit is a present that is not accepted? Accepting a present is not a work by which I earn the present, but it signifies laying hold of what is being offered.

Mark 16:16: He does not say: "He who is baptized and believes," but the reverse. Faith is the primary necessity; Baptism is something to which faith holds. Moreover, the Lord continues: *"But he who does not believe will be condemned."* This shows that even if a person could not have Baptism administered to himself, he would be saved, as long as he believed.

Acts 8:36-37: The only thing that Philip required was faith, as if he had said to the eunuch: "If you do not believe, being baptized will not benefit you at all." At our baptism it is not we that are performing a work, but God.

Gal. 3:26-27: Christ is put on in Baptism only if a person believes. The current interpretation is that anyone who is baptized has put on Christ; however, that is not what the apostle says, but: "As many *of you*," namely, of you who are "the children of God by faith." Such people, indeed, put on Christ in Baptism. An unbeliever who receives Baptism does not put on Christ, but keeps on the spotted garment of his sinful flesh.

At the institution of the Holy Supper the Lord says: "Take, eat; this is My body, *which* is given *for you*. Do this in remembrance of Me. Drink of it, all of you; this cup is the new testament in My blood, which is shed for you for the remission of sins." The Lord does not merely say: "This is My body," but He adds: "which is given for you"; He does not merely say: "This is My blood," but He adds: "Which is shed for you for the remission of sins." It is plain that He means to say: "The point of chief importance is that you believe that this body was given *for you* and that this blood was shed for the remission of *your* sins. That is what you must believe if you wish to derive the real blessing from this heavenly feast." By the additional remarks: "Do this in remembrance of Me," Christ means to say: "Do it in faith." Surely, He does not mean to say: "Think of Me when you partake of My body and blood. Do not forget Me altogether!" Whoever thinks that Christ merely admonished His disciples not to consign Him to oblivion does not know the Savior. The true remembrance of Christ consists in the *believing* reflection of the communicant: "This body was given for *me;* this blood was shed for the remission of *my* sins. That gives me confidence to approach the altar. To this truth I shall cling by faith and esteem my Savior's pledge very highly." For when God adds a visible pledge to His Word, who is there that dares to doubt that His Word is truth and His promise will certainly be fulfilled? As often as you go to Communion, have these words shine before your eyes: "Given for you"; "Shed for you for the remission of sins." If you fail to do this; if you imagine that by going to Communion you have once more done your duty and that God will regard your performance, your going to Communion is a damnable act. To go to Communion and eat the body of Christ and drink His blood with such a mind is an impudent action; but it is no impudence to hold fast to the word of His promise.

Rom. 4:11: We are told that Abraham believed before he was circumcised. Circumcision was intended to be merely a seal to him of the righteousness which he had by faith. It is an act of great kindness on the part of God, knowing how slow we are to believe even after we have become believers, to add external signs to His Word and to attach His promise to them; for the sacraments are connected with, and comprehended in, God's Word. The lustrous star that shines from out of the sacraments is the Word.

Our Church is frequently charged with teaching that Baptism procures for us *ex opere operato* adoption as children of God and the Lord's Supper *ex opere operato* the forgiveness of sins. It would be awful if we were to say first: "Man is not saved by works," and next: "However, by these two paltry works men are to obtain forgiveness of sins." True, many Lutherans determine by the almanac whether it is time for them to go to Communion again, because they imagine that going to Communion is a *work* which a Christian must perform and which he cannot afford to neglect. What is to urge a person to go to Communion is the promise of grace which God has attached to the visible signs in the Sacrament. If a person approaches the altar with faith in that promise, he will leave the Table of the Lord with a blessing in his heart.

The Lutheran Church speaks of the Sacraments in terms of such high esteem that fanatics become disgusted with it. The Lutheran Church holds to the word of the Lord: "He who believes and is baptized will be saved." That is the reason why it condemns all false teachers who say that Baptism is merely a ceremony by which a person is received into the church. According to Lutheran teaching, Baptism "works forgiveness of sins, delivers from death and the devil, and gives eternal salvation to all who believe, as the words and promises of God declare." The Lutheran Church maintains that Baptism is "the washing of regeneration and renewal in the Holy Spirit"; that the water in Baptism, as Peter says, "saves us"; and that those "who have been baptized into Christ have put on Christ." As regards the Lord's Supper, the Lutheran Church, resisting all attempts to mislead her into doubt, maintains the truth of the Lord's words when He says: "This is My body, which is given for you"; "This is My blood, which is shed for you." The Lutheran Church regards the holy sacraments as the most sacred, gracious, and precious treasure on earth. When God commands a sacramental act, He commands something upon which our salvation depends.

However, at no time has the Lutheran Church asserted that men are saved by the mere external use of the Sacraments. That is a teaching against which it has always raised its voice, which it has always combated and condemned.

The mere mechanical action of being baptized, if it is not accompanied by faith, will earn for man nothing but perdition. The truth of the matter is this: God is so kind that He not only has His mercy preached to men, but, in addition, tells them to come to the Sacrament, by which He seals to them the promise of grace, which they are only to believe. Likewise, a person who imagines that he obtains forgiveness of sins by the mere act of eating and drinking in the Lord's Supper is under a delusion. The body of Christ does not produce effects in a physical manner, as modernists claim when they say that it implants in man the seed of immortality. That idea is nothing but a dream of speculative theology, of which not a word is said in Scripture.

Moreover, just as Scripture does not teach that the mere outward act of hearing the Word saves anyone, just as little does it teach that the sacraments save thus. The mere symbol, placed before men's eyes, does not produce the salutary effect, but indicates what the Word proclaims. We baptize with water, which signifies that Baptism effects cleansing from sin, sanctification, regeneration, and renewal. What I am being told by means of preaching I behold in the external element of Baptism. The Word and the Sacrament produce the same effect in the heart.

Thesis XXII

In the eighteenth place, the Word of God is not rightly divided when a false distinction is made between a person's being awakened and his being converted; moreover, when a person's INABILITY *to believe is mistaken for his not* BEING PERMITTED *to believe.*

During the first half of the eighteenth century those who were guilty before others of this serious confusion of Law and Gospel were the so-called Pietists. These men were guilty of confounding Law and Gospel, namely, of keeping men away from Christ. They did this by making a false distinction between spiritual awakening and conversion; for they declared that, as regards the way of obtaining salvation, all men must be divided into three classes: 1. those still unconverted; 2. those who have been awakened, but are not yet converted; 3. those who have been converted.

This classification was utterly wrong. They would have been right if by people who have been awakened they had understood such persons as occasionally receive a powerful impression of the Word of God, of the Law and of the Gospel, but promptly stifle the impression, so that it is rendered ineffectual. For there are, indeed, men who can no longer continue to live in their carnal security, but suppress their unrest until God smites them again with the hammer of His Law and then makes them taste the sweetness of the Gospel. But the awakened persons to whom the Pietists referred are no longer to be numbered with the unconverted. According to Scripture we can assume only two classes: those who are converted and those who are not.

True, there are people who, when contrasted with true Christians, could be called awakened if they are not measured by the pattern of Holy Scripture: Herod Antipas, Felix, Festus, and Agrippa are examples.

People like these must not be numbered with the converted. But it is wrong to call them awakened. When Scripture speaks of awakening, it always means conversion. You must divide men into only two classes. The following passages will show you that by awakening Scripture means conversion: Eph. 5:14; 2:4-6; Col. 2:12.

100

However, Pietists object that a person who has not experienced a genuine, thorough contrition in his heart is not yet converted, but merely awakened. By thorough contrition they mean a contrition like that of David, who spent whole nights crying and weeping in his bed and walked almost bowed down with grief for days. Anyone who has not passed through these experiences, who has not yet been sealed with the Holy Spirit, is not quite assured of his state of grace and of salvation, is always wavering or shows himself uncharitable, lacking genuine patience and the proper willingness to serve his fellow-men; such a person, they claim, is certainly not a Christian, still unconverted and only awakened. This is an erroneous assumption. A person may have become a true Christian without experiencing the great and terrible anguish of David. For although David really passed through these experiences, the Bible does not say that everyone must pass through the same experiences and suffer in the same degree. As regards the sealing with the Holy Spirit, we read in Eph. 1:13: "In Him you also, who . . . have believed in Him, were sealed with the promised Holy Spirit." The sealing presupposes faith, although it may be a very weak faith, a faith that is constantly struggling with anxieties and doubts. God does not grant to everyone immediately boldness of faith and heroic courage. That this is the pure unadulterated truth can be seen in every record we have of people who were converted. Take, for instance, the first Pentecostal audience. These people were pricked in their hearts and asked the apostles: "Men and brethren, what shall we do?" Peter does not say to them: "Wait a while; first you must pass through a severe penitential struggle; you will have to wrestle with God and cry to Him for a long time until the Holy Spirit gives you the inward assurance that you have obtained grace and are saved." No; the apostle merely says: "Repent and be baptized," and immediately they received Baptism. "Repent" means: "Turn to your Lord Jesus, believe in Him, and as a seal of your faith receive Baptism, and everything will be right." Of these newly converted people we are told further on: "They devoted themselves to the apostles' teaching and fellowship, to the breaking of bread and the prayers" (Acts 2:37-38, 42). Hence they had become truly converted in a few moments.

The same observation meets us in the case of the Ethiopian treasurer. Philip merely says to him: "If you believe with all your heart, you may," namely, be baptized. When the treasurer answered: "I believe that Jesus Christ is the Son of God," Philip was fully satisfied; for he knew what the treasurer meant by his confession, namely, that he believed in the Messiah, God and man. After he had been baptized, they parted and probably never saw each other again. Philip was not worried in the least whether the man was actually converted; he was quite certain of his conversion because he had declared: "I believe that Jesus Christ is the Son of God." (Acts 8:37 ff.)

The jailer at Philippi was in despair because he feared he would be executed for allowing all his prisoners to escape. Paul arrested the jailer's hand as he was about to stab himself and cried: "Do not harm yourself, for we are all here." The jailer recalled the thoughts that had stirred his heart during the night while he had heard the prisoners whom he had subjected to such cruel treatment praising and glorifying God. Convicted of the wickedness of his heart and the magnitude of his sin, he fell at the apostles' feet, crying: "Men, what must I do to be saved?" Paul did not say to him: "That cannot be done tonight. We shall first have to give you instruction and ascertain the condition of your heart. We admit that you have been awakened, but you are far from being converted." No; he simply said: "Believe in the Lord Jesus, and you will be saved, you and your house" (Acts 16:27 ff.). The jailer believed and was filled with joy that he had become a believer. That is all Paul and Silas did. They left him, and when they had been given their liberty, they proceeded on their journey.

Try to find a single instance in the Scriptures where a prophet, apostle, or any other saint pointed the people another way to conversion, telling them that they could not expect to be converted speedily and that they would have to pass through such and such experiences. They always preached in a manner so as to terrify their hearers, and as soon as their hearers realized that there was no refuge for them, as soon as they condemned themselves and cried, "Is there no help for us?" they told them: "Believe in the Lord Jesus, and all will be well with you."

Fanatics declare that this is not the proper order of conversion. It is not the order of fanatics indeed, but it is God's order. As soon as the Gospel sounded in the ears of the persons aforementioned, it went through their hearts, and they became believers. We read that David, after receiving absolution, still had to suffer a great deal of anguish. But his penitential psalms are at the same time a confession of his assurance that God was gracious to him. It is sheer labor lost when a minister leads a person who has become alarmed over his sins a long way for months and years before that person can say, "Yes, I believe." Such a minister is a spiritual quack; he has not led that soul to Jesus, but to reliance on its own works. To every sinner who has become spiritually bankrupt and asks you: What must I do to be saved?

you must say: That is very simple: Believe in Jesus, your Savior, and all is well.

Consider that according to the Scriptures it is not at all difficult to be converted, but to remain in a converted state is difficult. Accordingly, it is a false interpretation to refer the words of the Savior: "Enter by the narrow gate," (Matt. 7:13) to repentance. Repentance is not a narrow gate through which a person has to squeeze. Repentance is something that God Himself must produce in a person. Any kind of repentance which man produces by his own effort is counterfeit and an abomination in the sight of God. We need not worry about our inability to produce repentance in ourselves. We must only apply to ourselves the Word of God, and we have the first part of repentance. After that an application of the unqualified Gospel will produce faith in us. All that a person has to do when he hears the Gospel is to accept it. *But this is immediately followed by an inward conflict. The error of false teachers in regard to this matter is that they place this conflict before conversion.* For such a conflict an unconverted person is not qualified. The conflict comes at a later stage, and it is severe. The narrow way is the cross which Christians have to bear, namely, that they have to mortify their own flesh, suffer ridicule, scorn, and ignominy heaped upon them by the world, fight against the devil, and renounce the world with its vanities, treasures, and pleasures. That is a task which causes many to fall away again soon after their conversion and to lose their faith. Wherever the Word of God is proclaimed with the manifestation of the Spirit and power of God, many more people are converted than we imagine. If we could look into the hearts of worshipers in a church where the Word is thus forcefully proclaimed and no works of men are mingled with the teaching of saving grace, we would observe many framing the resolution by the grace of God to become Christians; for they are convinced that the preacher is right. But many suppress these sensations the moment they leave the church and seek to persuade themselves that they have been listening to the discourse of a fanatic. Such persons harden themselves Sunday after Sunday and get into a most dangerous condition, past conversion. The Savior Himself says that many "receive the Word with joy" (Matt. 13:20), but smother the spouting germ when tribulations arise. This does not necessarily refer to severe diabolical afflictions, but, in general, to tedium as regards spiritual affairs, sluggishness in prayer, negligence in hearing the Word of God, contempt which Christians have to suffer from worldly men, etc. All these things may dissipate the impressions which had been made on the Christians' hearts. But does not the Lord say: "They *believe* for a while" (Luke 8:13)? Hence this second class of hearers, who quickly accept the Gospel, begin to *believe;* however, they do not permit the Word to strike root in their hearts, but at the next temptation to which they are exposed they again surrender to the world and their own flesh, and all that they had gained is lost.

Beware, then, of the illusion that men may become secure if they are told how quickly they may be led to repentance and conversion. On the contrary, consider the greatness of God's mercy. After a person has been converted, he must be told that henceforth he will have to be engaged in daily struggles and must think of making spiritual progress day by day, exercising himself in love, patience, and meekness and wrestling with sin. That is a lesson for converted Christians, who begin to cooperate with divine grace in them. But by the utterly abominable teaching of fanatics these spiritual conflicts are placed before conversion, and God is robbed of the honor due Him.

Where there is a spark of longing for mercy, there is faith; for faith is nothing else than longing for mercy. A person in whom this takes place is not merely awakened in the false sense of the word, but he is converted. It is remarkable that in Phil. 2:12-13 the apostle says, first: "Work out your own salvation with fear and trembling," and then continues: "For God is at work in you both to will and to work for His good pleasure." We are to work out our own salvation with fear and trembling for the very reason that our heavenly Father must do everything that is necessary for our salvation. That is what the apostle tells people who have been converted. A person who is hardened, blind, dead, cannot work out his own salvation, but a converted person can, and actually does, work out his own salvation. If he fails to do it, he is again stricken with spiritual blindness and relapses into spiritual death.

The so-called Pietists of former times and the preachers of the fanatical sects in our time not only made a false distinction between awakening and conversion and refused to regard those who were awakened as Christians, but they also mistook the inability to believe for not being permitted to believe.

When the Pietists had brought a person to the point where he considered himself a poor, miserable sinner, unable to help himself, and asked his minister what he must now do, the minister did not, like the apostles, answer him: "Believe in the Lord Jesus Christ, and you will be saved," but as a rule they told him the very opposite. They warned him against believing too soon and against thinking that, after having felt the effects of the Law, he might proceed to believe that his sins had been forgiven. They told him that his contrition must become more perfect, that he must feel contrite, not so much because his sins would call down upon him God's anger and hurl him into perdition, but because he loved God. Unless he could say that he felt sorry for having angered his merciful Father in heaven, his contrition was declared null and void. He was told that he must feel that God was beginning to be merciful to him; he must get so far that he could hear an inner voice telling him: "Take heart; your sins will be forgiven you; God will be merciful to you." He must continue struggling until his agony was over, and having rid himself of the love of sin and having been thoroughly converted, he might begin to take comfort.

The truth is, we are not to be converted *first* and *after that* believe; we are not first to have a sensation that we are in possession of grace; but without any feeling we are first to believe that we have received mercy, and after that will come the feeling of mercy, which God apportions to each according to His grace. Some persons are without feeling of grace for a long time. They behold nothing but darkness about them; they feel the hardness of their hearts and the powerful stirring and raging of evil, sinful lust within them. Accordingly, to point a person to the way of salvation, it is not the proper procedure to tell him that, even when he feels himself a poor, lost sinner, he may not yet believe himself saved.

True, no man can produce faith in himself; God must do that. A person may be in such a condition that he cannot believe, and God is not willing to bestow faith on him. A person who still considers himself sound and righteous cannot believe. "He who is sated loathes honey" (Prov. 27:7). A soul spiritually sated and surfeited tramples on the honey of evangelical consolation.

John 5:44: These words are unquestionably directed chiefly against the Pharisees. As long as a person is ambitious of honor, he cannot come to faith, because seeking one's honor is to be numbered with all other mortal sins. The Lord has declared that a person who simply will not quit a certain sin, *can* not believe in Him. The Law must first crush the sinner's heart before the sweet comfort of the Gospel is applied to him. But from this fact the inference must not be drawn that the sinner *may* not believe. It is forever true that any person may believe at any time. Even when he has fallen into the most grievous sin and, realizing suddenly that he has forsaken God, rises with a crushed heart, he may believe. Whoever tells him that he may not yet believe is either wicked or in this respect is still blind.

1 John 2:1-2: To tell a person that he may not believe is contrary to the perfect redemption of Christ from all sins and to the perfect reconciliation He has accomplished. The entire world has been reconciled. The wrath of God which hung lowering upon the whole world has been removed. Through Jesus Christ, God has become every man's Friend.

2 Cor. 5:14: Since Christ died, it is the same as if all men had suffered death for their sins, namely, the death which Christ died; it is the same as if all had atoned for their sins by their death. Now that the entire world has been redeemed and reconciled to God, is it not a horrible teaching to tell any person he may not believe that he has been reconciled and redeemed and has the forgiveness of sins? By that doctrine the completeness of redemption and reconciliation with God is shamefully denied.

Furthermore, this doctrine is contrary to the Gospel. After finishing the task of redemption and reconciliation, Christ said to His disciples: "Go into all the world and preach the Gospel to the whole creation" (Mark 16:15). To preach the Gospel means nothing else than bringing to all people the glad tidings that they have been redeemed, that heaven is opened to all, that all are made righteous, that perfect righteousness has been brought to them by Christ, and that men are but to come and enter by the gate of righteousness even as they shall one day enter by the gate of eternal salvation. Is it not horrible to tell men that they may not believe this? Everybody is to know that the Gospel is for him, that God has had the glad tidings brought to him in order that he may believe it and take comfort in it. If he refuses to believe it, he declares God and all His prophets and apostles liars. Is it not horrible to tell people who have learned by experience that they are poor, lost sinners and are still mired in sin, that, while God has indeed redeemed them, much still remains to be done on their part before they may believe and actually be redeemed? By this horrible teaching the sinner wants to share with God in the work of redemption. This is nothing short of blasphemy.

Nor does this harmonize with the fact that God has already declared in the presence of heaven and earth, of angels and men: "My Son has reconciled the world to Me. I have accepted His sacrifice. I am satisfied. He was your Surety, and I have set Him free. Therefore rejoice, for you have nothing to be afraid of." By the resurrection of Jesus Christ from the dead God has absolved the entire world of sinners from their sins. Is it not horrible for men to say that this is indeed a fact, but that a person may not yet believe it? Does not that mean to charge God with lying and to deny the resurrection of Christ from the dead?

Furthermore, this teaching is also contrary to the doctrine of absolution. Jesus Christ, after redeeming the entire world, has given His followers power to forgive everyone's sins. Some claim that the meaning of Christ is this: "When a minister notices that a person is in the proper condition, he may persuade him to believe that he has forgiveness of sins." But these are human imaginings; what the Lord says is simply this: "Your sins are forgiven." Moreover, this statement is readily comprehended by anyone who believes in the completeness of the redemption and reconciliation with God which Christ accomplished.

By the resurrection of Christ, God has declared that He is reconciled with all mankind and does not intend to inflict punishment on anybody. He has this fact proclaimed in all the world by His Gospel and, in addition, has commanded every minister of the Gospel to forgive men their sins, promising that He will do in heaven what the minister is doing on earth. The minister is not first to look up to heaven to ascertain what God is doing; he is merely to execute His orders on earth and forgive people's sins, relying on God's promise that He is forgiving them.

To some people this looks like a horrible doctrine, but it is the most comforting doctrine imaginable and is firmly established on the blood of God that was shed on the cross. Sin really has been forgiven, and all that God is now concerned about is that we believe this fact. We absolve men from their sins for no other purpose than to strengthen the faith of those who ask absolution in what they have heard proclaimed from the pulpit. Accordingly, none of them can say: "How can the minister know the condition of my heart? What is absolution to profit me when I am impenitent?" Answer: "Indeed, in that case it is of no benefit, but it is of benefit when it is believed. However, this is certain, that you have been absolved. Your eternal punishment will be all the more grievous because you did not believe the absolution which God Himself has pronounced to all sinners and which He has ordered His ministers to continue to pronounce to them."

This applies also to the sacraments. The water in Baptism saves us. When the Lord offers communicants the blessed bread and says: "This is My body, which is given for you," it is plain that He means to tell them they must believe or His body will not benefit them. A person who believes that Christ, by sacrificing His body, has paid for the communicant's sins can leave the altar rejoicing and exulting. When the Lord, offering the cup, says: "This cup is the new testament in My blood, which is shed for you for the remission of sins," He means to emphasize particularly the words "for the remission of sins" and to cause every communicant who believes them to shout inwardly with joy.

Lastly, mistaking inability to believe for not being permitted to believe is contrary to the practice of the apostles. Whenever a person showed the mark of a poor sinner, they told him to believe in the Lord Jesus Christ; they never asked him to wait until his condition had more fully developed. To his hearers on the first festival of Pentecost, Peter said that, while they had hated Christ, they were now believing in Him and should be baptized in His name. Remember also the instance of the jailer at Philippi which I have adduced so often. Fanatics, unless they plead ignorance of the apostles' practice, object to that practice because they claim that they would preach people into carnal security and ultimately into hell by that method. The apostles also had the sad experience of seeing that hypocrites had found their way into their congregations. I shall merely point to the instance of Simon the sorcerer. We are told: "Simon himself believed" (Acts 8:13), namely, before the eyes of men, but he was revealed later as an altogether wicked man. That did not cause the apostles to become "more cautious" and to resolve not always to invite people to believe in the Lord Jesus. For all the beautiful instances of sinners being invited by the apostles to believe immediately upon their confession of sin follow after the account of Simon the sorcerer.

It is, likewise, great folly to appeal to one's good intention. Pietists and many preachers among the fanatics have reasoned that, to make the conversion of their hearers thorough, they must not allow them to appropriate what does not yet belong to them because it would prove a false comfort to them. But this reasoning is a great piece of fanaticism. They ought to reflect that our heavenly Father is wiser than they. He knew very well that, when the consolations of the Gospel are imparted to all hearts, many will imagine that they, too, can believe them. But that is no reason why these consolations should be hushed up. We must not starve the children from fear that the dogs would get something of the children's food, but we are cheerfully to proclaim the universal grace of God freely and leave it to God whether people will believe it or misapply it.

Thesis XXIII

In the nineteenth place, the Word of God is not rightly divided when an attempt is made, by means of the demands or the threats or the promises of the Law, to induce the unregenerate to put away their sins and engage in good works and thus become godly; on the other hand, when an endeavor is made, by means of the commands of the Law rather than by the admonitions of the Gospel, to urge the regenerate to do good.

The attempt to make men godly by means of the Law and to induce even those who are already believers in Christ to do good by holding up the Law and issuing commands to them, is a very gross confounding of Law and Gospel. This is altogether contrary to the purpose which the Law is to serve after the Fall.

Jer. 31:31-34: While the Law was written into the hearts of men even before the Fall, it did not serve the purpose of making men godly; for man had been created godly and righteous in the sight of God. The only reason why men had to have the Law in their hearts was that they might know what is pleasing to God. No special command was needed to inform them on that point. They simply willed whatever was God-pleasing; their will was in perfect harmony with the will of God. This condition was changed by the Fall. True, God, after the exodus of the Israelites from Egypt, repeated the Law and reestablished a legal covenant with the Jews. However, what did the Lord tell them by the prophet Jeremiah? This, that the legal covenant had not improved their condition, because God had to force them to comply with His will — and forced obedience simply is no obedience. Accordingly, He speaks to them prophetically of a time when He will make an entirely different arrangement. This does not mean that the new arrangement was not in force even in the time of the Old Testament. The covenant, so far as it had been established with the Israelites, was a legal covenant. Yet during the time of this covenant the prophets were continually preaching the Gospel and pointing to the Messiah. Concerning the new covenant which God purposes to establish He says that He is not going to issue any commandments, but is going to write the Law directly into their mind and give them a new and pure heart, so that they shall not need to be plagued with the Law, with enforcements and urgings: You shall do this! You shall do that! because that will not help matters at all. We cannot fulfill the Law either. We are by nature carnal, and manifestations of the spirit are not forced from us by the Law. God says: "I will forgive their iniquity, and I will remember their sin no more." This is why the Law is written into our hearts. This means that what the Law could not effect is accomplished by the Gospel, by the message of the forgiveness of sins. All who were saved in the Old Testament were saved in no other way, as Peter expressly declared at the first apostolic council. Now, then, what are those doing who make such a perverse use of the Law in the time of the New Testament? They turn Christians into Jews, and that, Jews of the worst kind, who regard only the letter of the Law and not the promise of the Redeemer. Not only do they mingle the Law with the Gospel, but they substitute the Law for the Gospel.

Rom. 3:20: The Law has no other purpose than to reveal men's sins, not to remove them. Instead of removing them, it rather increases them; for when a person conceives evil lust in his heart, the Law calls to him: "You shall not covet." That causes man to regard God as cruel in demanding what man cannot accomplish. Thus the Law increases sin: it does not kill sin, but rather makes it alive. See also Rom. 7:7-13 and 2 Cor. 3:6.

How foolish, then, is a preacher who thinks that conditions in his congregation will improve if he thunders at his people with the Law and paints hell and damnation for them. That will not at all improve the people. Indeed, there is a time for such preaching of the Law in order to alarm secure sinners and make them contrite, but a change of heart and love of God and one's fellowmen is not produced by the Law. If anyone is prompted by the Law to do certain good works, he does them only because he is coerced, even as the Israelites had to be coerced by the covenant of the Law.

Gal. 3:2: The Galatians had allowed themselves to be misled into regarding Paul's preaching of salvation by faith, through the grace of Christ alone, as imperfect and hence as a dangerous doctrine by which a person might easily be led into perdition. Accordingly, they accepted the false prophets' doctrine of the Law. With great sadness Paul learned that these congregations were being disrupted and devastated by false teachers. Accordingly, he asked them the question in our text, his object being to remind them of the great change which had taken place in them when he preached to them the sweet Gospel of God's mercy. He called to their minds that they had received the Spirit, namely, the spirit of rest, of peace, of faith, of joy. He asks them: "What has become of the satisfaction you felt?" Yea, he says: "If possible, you would have plucked out your eyes and given them to me" (Gal. 4:15). So thoroughly had they been seized by the grace of God and so vividly had they perceived what a glorious, heavenly, precious doctrine Paul's was. They were transformed in heart, soul, and mind. The apostle wants them now to tell him whether they had received this new, heavenly peace in their hearts, this spiritual joy, this exceedingly great confidence, through the false teachers who had dragged them back into bondage under the Law. The apostle knew that the members of the congregations in Galatia went about sad and depressed, uncertain of their salvation. They were like men bewitched. They imagined, since salvation was such a great treasure, they must do something great for it, and their later teachers impressed this upon them as their duty. They regarded their misery, their unfitness for everything good, as something for which they had themselves to blame and not the false doctrine that had been put in their hearts.

The apostle is saying to you: <u>If you want to revive your future congregations and cause the Spirit of peace,</u> joy, faith, and confidence, the childlike spirit, the Spirit of soul-rest, to take up His abode among the members of your congregation, <u>you must, for God's sake, not employ the Law to bring that about.</u> If you find your congregations in the worst condition imaginable, you must, indeed, preach the Law to them, but follow it up immediately with the Gospel. You may not present the Law to them today and postpone preaching the Gospel to them until a later time. As soon as the Law has done its work, the Gospel must take its place.

This confounding of Law and Gospel, in the first place, is done by such as have arrived at the assurance of their state of grace only after much struggling and great anguish. They may have struggled for many years, refusing to be comforted, because they did not know the pure doctrine. When such people start out to proclaim the pure doctrine, they always intersperse their Gospel preaching with remarks which cause their hearers to say to themselves that the preacher must be a godly man, but that he does not know what poor men his hearers are; for they are sure that they cannot meet the requirements laid down by the preacher. These preachers represent the best type among errorists of this kind.

In the second place, this confounding of Law and Gospel occurs

111

when ministers become aware that all their Gospel-preaching is use-less because gross sins of the flesh still occur among their hearers. The preacher may come to the conclusion that he has preached too much Gospel to them and must adopt a different policy; he must hush the Gospel for a while and preach nothing but the Law, and conditions will improve. But he is mistaken; the people do not change. Preachers who have succeeded in abolishing certain evils by the preaching of the Law must not think that they have achieved something great. Even the most corrupt congregation can be improved, however, by nothing else than the preaching of the Gospel in all its sweetness. The reason why congregations are corrupt is invariably this, that its ministers have not sufficiently preached the Gospel to the people. It is not to be won-dered at that nothing has been accomplished by them; for the Law kills, but the Spirit, that is, the Gospel, makes alive.

Let no minister think that he cannot induce the unwilling to do God's will by preaching the Gospel to them and that he must rather preach the Law and proclaim the threatenings of God to them. If that is all he can do, he will only lead his people to perdition. Rather than act the policeman in his congregation, he ought to change the hearts of his members in order that they may without constraint do what is pleasing to God with a glad and cheerful heart. A person who has a real understanding of the love of God in Christ Jesus is astonished at its fire, which is able to melt anything in heaven and on earth. The moment he believes in this love he cannot but love God and from grati-tude for his salvation do anything from love of God and for His glory.

Thesis XXIV

In the twentieth place, the Word of God is not rightly divided when the unforgivable sin against the Holy Ghost is described in a manner as if it could not be forgiven because of its magnitude.

Only the Law condemns sin, the Gospel absolves the sinner from all sins without an exception. The prophet writes: "Though your sins are like scarlet, they shall be as white as snow; though they are red like crimson, they shall become like wool" (Is. 1:18). The apostle Paul writes (Rom. 5:20): "Where sin increased, grace abounded all the more."

Matt. 12:30-32 states, to begin with, that all blasphemy against the Father and the Son shall be forgiven; only the blasphemy against the Holy Ghost shall not be forgiven. Now, it is certain that the Holy Spirit is not a more glorious and exalted person than the Father and the Son, but He is coequal with them. Accordingly, the meaning of this passage cannot be that the unforgivable sin is blasphemy against the person of the Holy Spirit; for blasphemy against the Father and the Son is exactly the same sin. The blasphemy to which our text refers is directed *against the office,* or operation, of the Holy Spirit; whoever spurns the office of the Holy Spirit, his sin cannot be forgiven. The office of the Holy Spirit is to call men to Christ and to keep them with Him.

The person committing this sin *"speaks* against the Holy Ghost." This shows that the sin in question is not committed by blasphemous thoughts that arise in the heart. Not infrequently Christians imagine they have committed this sin when they are visited with horrid thoughts of which they cannot rid themselves. Our Lord Christ foresaw this, and for that reason He informed us that the blasphemy against the Holy Ghost that is not forgiven must have been uttered by the mouth.

Mark 3:28-30: Here is the record of an actual blasphemy against the Holy Ghost. When Christ cast out devils, the Pharisees declared this operation of the Holy Spirit a work of the devil. They were convinced that it was a divine work, but since the Savior had rebuked them for their hypocrisy they conceived a deadly hatred against Christ, and that incited them to blasphemy against the Holy Ghost.

To declare a *work* of the Holy Ghost a work of the devil when one is convinced that it is a work of the Holy Ghost is blasphemy against the Holy Ghost. There are no Christians that do not occasionally resist the operations of divine grace and then try to persuade themselves that they were only chasing away gloomy thoughts. This doctrine warns us that, if we wish to be saved, we must yield promptly to the operation of the Holy Spirit as soon as we feel it and not resist it. For in the next stage the person who resists may find himself saying: "This operation is not by the Holy Spirit." The following stage will be that he begins to hate the way by which God wants to lead him to salvation, and ultimately he will blaspheme that way.

Unless the Holy Spirit brings us to faith, we shall never attain it. Whoever rejects the Holy Spirit is beyond help, even by God. God wants the order maintained which He has ordained for our salvation. He brings no one into heaven by force. On the occasion to which our text refers Christ had just healed the man with the withered hand and had driven out a devil. Everybody saw that the power of God was making an inroad into the kingdom of Satan. But the reprobates who stood by said: "Ah! Beelzebub is in this Jesus; that is why He can cast out inferior devils." The very action which they had witnessed, the works and the words of Christ, showed that He was arrayed against the devil and was destroying the devil's kingdom. It was wholly out of reason to imagine that the devil would help Christ in that work.

Heb. 6:4-8: It is a characteristic of the sin against the Holy Ghost that *the person who has committed it cannot be restored to repentance.* That is simply impossible. It is not God who puts man into this condition, but the sinner by his own fault produces this state of irretrievable impenitence. When this condition has reached a certain degree, God ceases to operate on the person. The curse has settled upon him, and there is no further possibility for the person to be saved. Why? Because he cannot be induced to repent.

1 John 5:16 contains important information for us, but we cannot act upon it. For we can say of no person before his death that he has committed the sin against the Holy Ghost. Even when his mouth utters blasphemies, we do not know to what extent his heart is implicated, or whether the phenomenon is not perhaps an operation of the devil, or whether he is acting in great blindness, and whether he may not be renewed unto repentance. The Christians in the days of the apostles had the gift to discern the spirits. Accordingly, St. John here

means to say: "When you see that God has ceased to be gracious to such or such an individual who has committed this sin, you are not to wish either that God should be gracious to him, and you are to cease praying for him." Neither may we say to God: "Save those who have committed the sin against the Holy Ghost."

This is a shocking statement, and yet it contains a great comfort. Someone may come to you and say: "I am a wretched man – I have committed the sin against the Holy Ghost. I am quite certain of it." The afflicted may tell you of the evil he has done, the evil he has *spoken,* and the evil he has thought. It may really look as if he had blasphemed the Holy Ghost. Now remember the weapon which Heb. 6 furnishes for attacking a case like this: That person is not at all rejoicing over what he tells you; it is all so awfully horrid to him. This shows that God has at least begun to lead him to repentance; all that he need do is to lay hold of the promise of the Gospel. When you ask him whether he has been doing all those evil things intentionally, he may affirm that involuntarily because Satan makes him affirm the question. When you ask him whether he wishes he had not done those evil things, he will answer: "Yes, indeed; these things are causing me the most awful worry." That is a sure sign that God has begun the work of repentance in that person. A case like this is indeed not to be treated lightly; the sufferer must be shown that, since there is in him the beginning of repentance, he has an indubitable proof that he has not committed the sin against the Holy Ghost. In general, when preaching on this subject, the minister must aim at convincing his hearers that they have not committed this sin rather than warn them not to commit it. To a person who has really committed this sin preaching is of no benefit. Whoever is sorry for his sins and craves forgiveness should be told that he is a dear child of God, but is passing through a terrible tribulation.

The sin is not unpardonable because of its magnitude – for the apostle, as we heard, has distinctly declared: "Where sin increased, grace abounded all the more" – but because the person committing this sin rejects the only means by which he can be brought to repentance, faith, and steadfastness in faith.

As regards people who are distressed because they think they have committed the sin against the Holy Ghost, they would not feel distressed if they really had committed that sin and were in that awful condition of heart, but they would find their constant delight in blaspheming the Gospel. However, Christians in distress still have faith, and the Spirit of God is working in them; and if the Spirit of God is working in them, they have not committed the sin against the Holy Ghost.

An excellent exposition of this matter is found in *Baier's* Latin *Compend of Positive Theology.* He says in Part II, chap. III, sec. 24: "The most grievous of all actual sins, which is called the sin against the Holy Ghost, consists in a malicious renunciation and blasphemous and obstinate assaults upon the heavenly truth which had once upon a time been known by the person committing this sin."

A person who has committed the sin against the Holy Ghost is condemned not so much on account of this sin as rather on account of his unbelief. Unbelief is the general cause and malicious and constant vilification of the truth the particular cause of his damnation.

Thesis XXV

In the twenty-first place, the Word of God is not rightly divided when the person teaching it does not allow the Gospel to have a general predominance in his teaching.

Law and Gospel are confounded and perverted for the hearers of the Word, not only when the Law predominates in the preaching, but also when Law and Gospel, as a rule, are equally balanced and the Gospel is not predominant in the preaching.

Luke 2:14: The heavenly preacher gave us an illustration of how we are to preach. True, we have to preach the Law, only, however, as a preparation for the Gospel. The ultimate aim in our preaching of the Law must be to preach the Gospel. Whoever does not adopt this aim is not a true minister of the Gospel.

Mark 16:15-16: Christ tells His apostles to go into all the world and preach the Gospel to every creature. The mere term *Gospel* serves notice on them that their message must be a message of joy. Lest they think that this word is so infinitely great that nobody will grasp its meaning, He adds these words immediately: "He who believes and is baptized shall be saved," to let them know that this is what He understands by the word *Gospel*. He proceeds: "He who does not believe will be condemned." This, too, is a sweet word; for He does not say: "He that has sinned much for a long time shall be damned," but states no other reason for man's damnation than his unbelief. No matter what a person's character is and how grievously he has sinned, nothing in his past record shall damn him. But, naturally, when a person refuses to believe the words of Jesus, he has to go to perdition. The alarming reference to damnation is merely to prompt men to accept His gracious message and not to put it from them. These last words of the Lord should not be emphasized thus: "He who does *not* believe will be condemned," but thus: "He who does not *believe* will be condemned." He means to say: "Your damnation has already been removed from you; your sin has been taken away; hell has already been overcome for you. I have rendered a sufficient atonement for everything. It is now for you to *believe* this, and you will be saved forevermore."

1 Cor. 15:3: Do not merely listen to this statement of the apostle, but think of the time when you will be the pastor of a congregation and make a vow to God that you will adopt the apostle's method, that you will not stand in your pulpits sad-faced, as if you were bidding men to come to a funeral, but like men that go wooing a bride or announcing a wedding. If you do not mingle Law with the Gospel you will always enter your pulpit with joy. People will notice that you are filled with joy because you are bringing the blessed message of joy to your congregation. They will furthermore notice that wonderful things are happening among them. Alas! many ministers do not meet with these wonderful experiences; their hearers remain sleepy; their misers stay stingy. What is the reason? Not sufficient Gospel has been preached to them. The people who go to church in America really want to hear the Word of God. We are living in a free country, where it is nobody's concern whether one goes to church or not. In accordance with God's will it should be the preacher's aim to proclaim the Gospel to his hearers till their hearts are melted, till they give up their resistance and confess that the Lord has been too strong for them, and henceforth they wish to abide with Jesus. It is not sufficient for you to be conscious of your orthodoxy and your ability to present the pure doctrine correctly. These are, indeed, important matters; however, no one will be benefited by them if you confound Law and Gospel. The very finest form of confounding both occurs when the Gospel is preached *along with* the Law, but is not the predominating element in the sermon. The preacher may think that he has proclaimed the evangelical truth quite often. His hearers, however, remember only that on some occasions he preached quite comfortingly and told them to believe in Jesus Christ. Without telling them how to attain to faith in Christ, your hearers will be spiritually starved to death if you do not allow the Gospel to predominate in your preaching. They will be spiritually underfed because the bread of life is not the Law, but the Gospel.